HEROES
IN THE SKIES

HEROES
IN THE SKIES

AMERICAN AVIATORS IN
WORLD WAR II

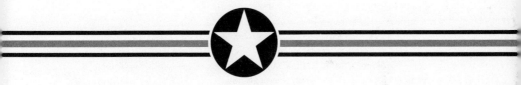

IAN DARLING

STERLING
New York

STERLING
New York

An Imprint of Sterling Publishing Co., Inc.
1166 Avenue of the Americas
New York, NY 10036

ISBN 978-1-4549-1749-6

Distributed in Canada by Sterling Publishing Co., Inc.
c/o Canadian Manda Group, 664 Annette Street
Toronto, Ontario, M6S 2C8, Canada
Distributed in the United Kingdom by GMC Distribution Services
Castle Place, 166 High Street, Lewes, East Sussex, BN7 1XU, United Kingdom
Distributed in Australia by NewSouth Books
45 Beach Street, Coogee, NSW 2034, Australia

For information about custom editions, special sales, and premium and corporate purchases,
please contact Sterling Special Sales at 800-805-5489 or specialsales@sterlingpublishing.com.

Manufactured in the United States of America

2   4   6   8   10   9   7   5   3   1

www.sterlingpublishing.com

A complete list of photo credits appears on pages 281-282.

★ ★ ★

To the men and women who helped America

during World War II and in the conflicts

that have occurred since then

★ ★ ★

CONTENTS

President Truman announces the end of World War II in Europe on May 8, 1945.

FOREWORD

ON THE MORNING OF DECEMBER 7, 1941, THE IMPERIAL JAPANESE
Navy attacked the American Pacific Fleet at Pearl Harbor,
pulling the United States into a war that by that point
had claimed millions of lives already. Before its end, the war claimed
millions more and saw the only wartime use of nuclear weapons, an
attack ordered by my grandfather, President Harry S. Truman. Many
of the men and women in this book didn't expect to be warriors. They
didn't see themselves as heroes. They just had a job to do.

Jim Landis witnessed Japanese aircraft firing torpedoes at the USS
Utah, moored near Ford Island. An aviation machinist mate, Landis
responded quickly to the surprise attack. He ran to an SBD Dauntless
dive bomber to fire from the ground at the attacking planes as they flew
above a runway.

Sergeant Frank Buschmeier didn't panic when an anti-aircraft shell
blew a twelve-by-six-foot hole in the fuselage of his B-17 as it flew over
the English Channel. He contacted the pilot, Second Lieutenant John
Gibbons, to report, "The whole damn radio room is gone!" Despite that
massive damage, Buschmeier and the rest of the crew decided to stay
in the plane rather than bail out over England. Everyone believed their
pilot could land a damaged plane.

Second Lieutenant George McGovern knew that members of the crew on the B-24 Liberator he was piloting had become agitated after realizing the aircraft's brakes and wing flaps might not work. McGovern, who would be the Democratic Party's candidate for president in 1972, calmed his men with a few well-chosen words. As Ian Darling points out, even those members of his crew who never would have voted for him respected his leadership. The war affected McGovern's long-term thinking. Although not a pacifist, he said, "War should always be regarded as a last recourse."

Lieutenant Junior Grade George H. W. Bush, who was shot down over the Pacific, felt the same. As director of the CIA and president, Bush valued teamwork, never forgetting that his comrades went out of their way to rescue him.

Regardless of whether you believe the decision to use atomic weapons against Japan was right or wrong, necessary or not, my grandfather made it, first and foremost, to save Americans like Landis, Buschmeier, McGovern, and Bush. He had fought in World War I and had tremendous respect for soldiers. He had watched too many of them die.

Thankfully the world has gone more than seventy years without being embroiled in a global conflict as massive as World War II. We must hope that it was the last of its kind. We must do what we can to make sure it was the last of its kind.

Clifton Truman Daniel
Chicago

INTRODUCTION

WHAT MAKES A HERO

M Y BRITISH-BORN FATHER SPOKE WITH GREAT RESPECT ABOUT
the Americans he met in the Army Air Forces during
World War II. A sergeant in the Royal Air Force, he often
remarked that American officers acted differently than British officers.
The Americans, he said, took off their jackets and did the heavy work
with the enlisted men, but British officers often stood aside to let the
lower ranks do the hard, physical work. He had plenty of opportunity
to observe the differences because one of his tasks during the war was
helping Americans move onto bases in England that the Royal Air Force
had lent to them.

As I wrote this book, I thought often of my dad. He, along with
millions of men and women in the Allied countries, knew that America's
decision to join the fight after the Japanese attacked Pearl Harbor would
prove one of the most significant events of the entire war and perhaps
the century. As had been the case during World War I, America's participation virtually ensured that Germany couldn't defeat the Allies—even

if victory took a long, belabored time and claimed millions of lives on both sides.

When I interviewed the aviators in this book, I saw in them what my father saw in the Americans he met: determination to do what had to be done to win a war that America hadn't started but wanted to finish as quickly as possible. *Heroes in the Skies* shows what individual fliers did and how they felt as they fought against Imperial Japan and Nazi Germany in the air. Any branch of the armed services—and the Army Air Forces didn't become the independent US Air Force until after the war—fights only as well as the men and women who serve in it, and these men and women served valiantly.

Yes, the attack on Pearl Harbor changed everything. Before the attack, America stood divided between isolationists loudly demanding continued neutrality and the pro-war faction that angrily clamored over the looming hostilities overseas growing closer and stronger. The Japanese planes that wrought havoc in Hawaii—still a federal territory and not yet a state—united Americans as nothing else could have done. Ardent to join the war effort virtually from the moment they heard the news about the attack, the men and women in the following pages let nothing stand in their way to prevent them from defending their country and their comrades. They personified the American spirit when they climbed aboard their various aircraft—from two-seat fighters to B-17 Flying Fortresses—and executed their missions, be they simple ferrying or scouting flights or long-haul raids over vast expanses of ocean.

In writing *Heroes in the Skies*, I decided to do more than tell just the lighthearted stories that veterans might recall with their old war buddies over a drink in a bar. I set out to show that, when motivated, Americans, both individually and collectively, can accomplish amazing feats that even they might not have thought possible. These fliers never imagined that they would achieve what they did during the war, and virtually all said that they were just doing their jobs. They didn't expect or even want to become heroes. We regard them as such today because they risked their lives from the moment they donned their uniforms until that incredible, almost unbelievable moment when the war ended. That's what makes a hero.

Just as these aviators helped win the war, so too did the war influence them. They took the valuable lessons they had learned in the heat of combat and applied them to the rest of their lives. Many of them here divulge those pearls of wisdom gleaned in battle that continued to guide them as they became politicians, military lifers, and businessmen—all keenly aware of how different the world might look had they not done their part.

As a Canadian, I decided to write about American aviators who survived the harrowing ordeals that you're about to relive because Americans and Canadians have much in common. We share more than a continent and a border. Even apart from our joint colonial beginnings, we have many values—including a dedication to the traditions of democracy and the rule of law—in common. Along with the other Allied nations and territories of the world, Americans and Canadians fought together in two world wars to defend these values. The fliers in *Heroes in the Skies* and the many others whose stories remain untold, including many of our parents and grandparents, risked their lives during World War II to ensure that today we can live in countries where these values reign supreme.

After President Truman authorized the detonation of atomic bombs on Japan, the war ended, of course. The veterans whose stories appear in this book undoubtedly would agree with the opinion expressed by President Truman's grandson Clifton Truman Daniel in the foreword: We must do what we can to make sure it stands as the last global conflict.

Every day we're losing veterans who served during the war. They might say in their later years that they were the fortunate ones because they survived the war when many of their comrades did not. Nevertheless, we must count ourselves the fortunate ones because we benefit from what the veterans did. For this, we must thank them before all of what journalist Tom Brokaw has called the Greatest Generation slips away.

With many of the veterans now in their nineties, the commemorative ceremonies on December 7, 2016, to mark the seventy-fifth anniversary of the attack on Pearl Harbor likely will provide the last opportunity that we'll have to honor their dwindling ranks. But in many cases, we still have time. Visit your parents and grandparents who fought in the war, and ask them to talk about their wartime ordeals. Write down their stories, do what you can to preserve them, and share them with family and friends. Aside from invaluably recording firsthand accounts of one of the most significant periods of twentieth-century history, these stories will provide us and future generations with inspiration to overcome whatever challenges lie in the years ahead.

We owe it to the veterans who died while serving the greater good, those we have lost in the years since then, and those still among us. We also owe it to them to think carefully about the best ways to keep both America and the world a peaceful, free place. They and all of their comrades risked their lives precisely so that we could hold those discussions and debates. We owe them so much more, but at the very least we owe them that.

SHOCKWAVES

JAMES LANDIS
Aviation Machinist Mate, 2nd Class
Bombing Squadron 2
US Navy

A FTER A LONG OVERNIGHT FLIGHT TO HAWAII, THE RADIO OPER-
ator on Lieutenant Harry Brandon's B-17 saw a strange sight.
About 7:30 a.m., he noticed a large number of planes flying
from the north. Because they were riding the horizon, he couldn't identify them. Speaking on the intercom, the radio operator expressed
surprise at that many American planes flying on a Sunday morning.
Brandon, the pilot; Aviation Cadet Harold Snider, the navigator; and
the rest of the crew agreed with him. There was something odd about
those planes.

It was December 7, 1941.

Brandon called the control tower at Hickam Field on Oahu to
inform the air base of the approaching aircraft, but the tower was too
far away for him to make contact, and soon the mysterious planes flew
out of sight.

The 38th Reconnaissance Squadron had landed at Hickam
Field earlier that morning. Brandon's crew, members of the 88th
Reconnaissance Squadron, were still on their fourteen-hour flight from
Hamilton Army Airfield, near San Francisco, also to Hickam. Because
of mounting tensions with the Japanese in the Pacific, a senior officer
had warned the two squadrons before their departure that a military
conflict could erupt while they were en route. The squadrons were stopping in Hawaii only to rest and refuel. After a day's pause, they had
orders to fly to Clark Field in the Philippines, near Manila.

Despite the senior officer's warning, the machine guns on the B-17s
weren't made operational because Pearl Harbor was considered a safe
destination, too far from Japan for imperial forces to attack.

★

AS THE B-17S OF THE 88TH FLEW TOWARD HAWAII, JIM LANDIS STOOD NEAR SBD Dauntless dive bombers and other planes parked near the runway at Ford Island in Pearl Harbor. The aircraft normally sat on the USS *Lexington*, an aircraft carrier based there. The carrier, however, had left several planes on Ford Island when it departed on December 5 to deliver eighteen aircraft to a Marine Corps squadron on Midway Island.

Landis, twenty-one years old, hailed from Jackson, Michigan. He had joined the Navy in 1939 and was serving as an aviation machinist mate second class. He expected to enjoy a pleasant, peaceful Sunday morning. He had handed pistols to several crewmembers of the *Lexington* who had stayed on the island to guard the planes in case they encountered saboteurs. He completed his assignment shortly before 8 a.m. and strolled toward a hangar.

Then suddenly, near the northwest side of Ford Island, an explosion ripped through the harbor. The USS *Utah*, a training ship, lay moored about one hundred yards offshore in the berth normally used by the *Lexington*. Landis ran five hundred yards to the edge of the island. Planes had fired torpedoes at the *Utah*, striking it, and it was keeling over slowly. In shock, Landis watched the *Utah* helplessly for a few minutes.

Because it was Sunday morning, many of the sailors on Ford Island were still sleeping. Of those who weren't, some sought shelter in hangars, but Landis ran several hundred yards to the closest aircraft, one of the SBD Dauntless bombers, because he knew they were armed.

An explosion ripped through the harbor.

As he ran, aircraft flying just above the runway fired their machine guns at the planes on the ground. Landis recognized the red circles on the wings of the attacking planes. They represented the rising sun. Japan had launched a surprise attack on the United States of America.

The Japanese planes fired at sailors from the *Utah* who were swimming ashore through water quickly slicking with oil. After about ten minutes, the *Utah* capsized.

Landis tried to climb into an SBD from the right, but in the confusion he had forgotten that the canopy latch lay on the left side. As he reached his left arm over the canopy to open the latch, a bullet from a Japanese plane pierced the palm of his hand. He could see through the hole—but the adrenaline pumping through his body as he focused on the enemy aircraft kept Landis from feeling most of the pain. He opened the canopy and climbed into the Dauntless. With both hands, he lifted the heavy ammunition belt, fed the bullets into the twin .30-caliber machine guns, and squeezed the trigger.

Landis returned fire for about twenty minutes, until the enemy aircraft finally departed. The Japanese had damaged or destroyed thirty-three of seventy-two aircraft on Ford Island. Landis didn't know whether he had shot down any enemy planes. Still numb to the pain of his wound, he climbed out of the SBD.

★

AS LIEUTENANT BRANDON FLEW CLOSER TO OAHU, HE INTERCOMMED THE crew that he was going to fly by Diamond Head. Brandon knew his crewmates would like to see the volcanic mountain, a popular tourist site about ten miles southeast of the Hickam base. The crew saw Diamond

"We're under attack!" said the controller.

Head clearly. Then Brandon tried contacting the Hickam tower again. Again, no one responded.

But a few minutes later, the tower contacted Brandon. "We're under attack!" said the controller. "Land the best way you can."

At that moment, the entire crew realized where the planes that the radio operator had seen earlier had been going.

Snider, the twenty-four-year-old navigator, saw Japanese aircraft bombing Pearl Harbor. He also spotted three Japanese Zeros attacking the B-17 ahead of their aircraft, and then their own. Bullets started a fire in the forward B-17, flown by Captain Raymond Swenson. It split in two immediately after landing on a runway. Lieutenant William Schick, a flight surgeon on board, was killed in the crash.

With a few bullet holes in his plane but no casualties, Brandon approached the runway after Swenson's B-17 had landed. Brandon didn't say anything to the crew about the attack. He didn't have to say anything. Everyone knew what was happening. Everyone knew their B-17 was defenseless.

Brandon had to stay to the right side of the runway to avoid hitting the two parts of Swenson's plane. Their B-17 stopped safely at the end of the runway. The crew quickly exited the plane and ran to a nearby dry creek, hoping it would provide some protection. They weren't safe, however. The three Zeros circled around and fired at them. Snider responded to the ordeal calmly. In the creek, he prayed for divine assistance, and no bullet struck him.

★ HEROES IN THE SKIES ★

Other Japanese aircraft were firing and dropping bombs on various targets at the Hickam base: parked planes, the mess hall, the theater. Some of the men on base died in their sleep when the Japanese attacked the barracks.

After the attack, Brandon's crew had their B-17 refueled and machine guns installed. When their aircraft was ready, Snider and a crewmate told a general that their crew and plane were battle-ready.

"You know we're not at war," the general replied, "so there's no way I can send you back out there."

Snider had grown up in Robinson, Illinois, and joined the Army Air Corps in 1939 after graduating from an engineering course. If the United States wasn't involved in a war, he thought it was dealing with a pretty good imitation of one.

Ten other B-17s came down at various locations on Oahu, but not all at air bases designed for them. One landed on a golf course. Mechanics were able to repair most of the planes, including the one on the golf course; it later flew to Hickam.

In the short run, the Japanese forces were successful. By attacking early on a Sunday morning, they caught Americans in Hawaii either literally or figuratively sleeping. It later emerged that an officer on duty ignored a warning signal from a newly installed radar unit on Oahu about planes coming from the north.

A total of 353 Japanese planes in two waves damaged or destroyed

---

An officer on duty ignored a warning signal about planes coming from the north.

---

a large part of America's Pacific Fleet, as well as many aircraft and military buildings on Oahu. The attack left 2,403 Americans dead and 1,178 wounded.

Japanese military officers such as Commander Mitsuo Fuchida, who coordinated the first wave, and Lieutenant Commander Kakuichi Takahashi, who led the dive bombers who attacked Ford Island and Hickam Field, undoubtedly had accomplished their goals. But President Franklin Roosevelt predicted the following day that the date of their attack would "live in infamy." In his speech to a joint session of Congress, Roosevelt revealed that the Japanese had attacked not only Oahu but also Malaya, Hong Kong, Guam, the Philippines, Wake Island, and Midway Island. "The facts of yesterday speak for themselves," he said. "The people of the United States have already formed their opinions and well understand the implications to the very life and safety of our nation."

Shortly after Roosevelt finished speaking, Congress declared war on Japan. Three days later, the conflict expanded across the globe when Germany declared war on the United States.

★

AFTER JIM LANDIS CLIMBED OUT OF THE SBD, NAVY MEN BROUGHT HIM from Ford Island to the hospital at Pearl Harbor. He joined the ranks of many men taken to the hospital that morning. The medical staff there, like the sailors, weren't prepared for war, but they had enough morphine on hand to prevent Landis from feeling the pain of the bullet hole in his left palm.

Doctors examined his injury and feared he would lose the hand, but they were able to rebuild it, stretching various tissues and then skin over the wound. Landis lost only some feeling in his ring finger.

The hospital soon transferred Landis to the USS *Solace*, a hospital ship moored in the harbor. From the *Solace*, he saw what remained of the USS *Arizona*. A bomb dropped by a Japanese plane had triggered an explosion in the battleship's ammunition storage area that killed 1,177 sailors and marines. Observing the wreckage, he and the other men recuperating on the *Solace* felt impatient. They wanted to rejoin their comrades and help America defeat Japan as soon as possible.

While Landis recovered, the *Lexington* returned to Pearl Harbor without delivering the Marines' planes to Midway Island. (Those eighteen planes later flew to Midway directly.) The medical staff on the *Solace* declared Landis fit for duty once more in February 1942. Released, Landis returned to the *Lexington*. He served as a plane captain, performing mechanical work on SBDs and sometimes flying as a gunner and radio operator in the two-seater plane.

Landis was aboard the *Lexington* on May 8, 1942, when the carrier participated in the Battle of the Coral Sea, off the northeast coast of Australia. The Navy wanted to weaken Japanese forces to prevent them from taking additional territory in the Pacific. During the battle, enemy aircraft bombed and torpedoed the *Lexington*, starting multiple fires on the carrier. At about 5 p.m., Captain Frederick Sherman, the commanding officer, ordered his crew to abandon ship.

Several Navy ships approached the *Lexington* to take on men from the carrier. Armed with a pair of binoculars and a life preserver, Landis climbed down a rope on the side of the *Lexington* at midship. Halfway down, he saw that the USS *Anderson*, a nearby destroyer, already was pulling away. He let go of the rope, dropped into the water, swam toward the *Anderson*, and climbed aboard.

Working planes on the *Lexington* flew to another carrier. Then, to prevent the Japanese from commandeering it later, an American destroyer fired additional torpedoes to sink it.

After a few days on the *Anderson*, Landis transferred to other ships and sailed to San Diego. He returned to Michigan for a brief leave, and, when he reported back for duty, the Navy sent him to Guadalcanal, an island in the Solomon Islands, to help build an airport.

★

HAROLD SNIDER, THE NAVIGATOR ON Brandon's B-17, flew more than one hundred combat missions in the Pacific Theater. In November 1942, he returned to the United States to become a navigational instructor. He won several medals, including the Silver Star and the Distinguished Service Cross. In July 1943, at Casper Army Airfield in Wyoming, where Snider was based, General Henry "Hap" Arnold congratulated him for participating in an attack on a Japanese army base at Manila Municipal Airport that killed several senior Japanese officials.

General "Hap" Arnold (left) congratulates Harold Snider at Casper Army Airfield in Wyoming in 1943 for participating in an attack on a Japanese army base that killed several senior Japanese officials.

Harold Snider in 2012

Bullet holes from the attack on Pearl Harbor in a window of Hangar 79 on Ford Island in Pearl Harbor.

After the war, Harold Snider worked as a petroleum engineer around the world before retiring to Phoenix. He died in 2015 at age ninety-seven.

★

MITSUO FUCHIDA, THE JAPANESE AVIATOR WHO LED THE FIRST WAVE OF planes that attacked Pearl Harbor, survived the war and later became an evangelist. Moved by Christianity's emphasis on forgiveness, Fuchida sometimes preached in the United States. He died in Japan in 1976.

"I hate surprises," he said.

★

AFTER THE WAR, LANDIS REMAINED IN THE NAVY UNTIL HIS RETIREMENT in 1970 as a senior chief petty officer. But he never discovered whether he hit any Japanese planes when he fired from the SBD on that fateful day in 1941.

He twice went back to Pearl Harbor. On his first visit, in 2006, emotion overcame him when he saw the wreckage of the *Utah*, which remains in the harbor. For Landis and many others who witnessed the destruction of that day and those that followed, the *Utah* symbolizes the start of a fierce war in which countless men fought and often died together.

In 2011, Landis returned to attend the ceremony marking the seventieth anniversary of the attack. Ford Island still bears witness to that assault. Strafing marks made by machine-gun bullets still exist in what were seaplane ramps, and bullet holes mark windows in Hangar 79, now part of the Pacific Aviation Museum.

SBD 2106, in which Landis sometimes flew, later saw service in training aviators in Illinois. In 1943, a pilot had to ditch the aircraft in Lake Michigan. It sank but was recovered in 1994. Today the aircraft stands on display at the National Naval Aviation Museum in Pensacola, Florida. The museum also displays the life jacket that Landis was wearing when the *Lexington* sank.

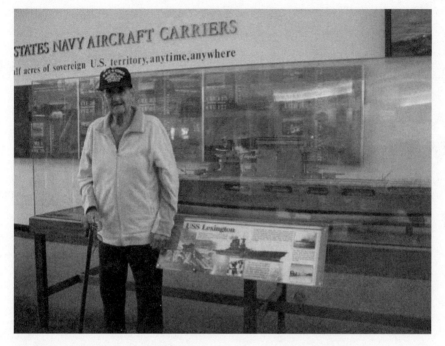

Jim Landis stands in front of a model of the USS *Lexington* at the National Naval Aviation Museum in Pensacola, Florida, in 2012.

At his home in Pensacola, Landis said that his experience at Pearl Harbor taught him the importance of being prepared for the unthinkable.

"I hate surprises," he said.

He died in 2014 at the age of ninety-four.

THE VOLUNTEER

THOMAS GRIFFIN
Second Lieutenant
34th Bomb Squadron
17th Bombardment Group
US Army Air Forces

A GLENN MILLER RECORD WAS PLAYING WHEN A NEIGHBOR delivered the shocking news on Sunday, December 7, 1941. Second Lieutenant Tom Griffin was relaxing with friends, but he knew instantly that the attack would affect him personally. A navigator at the Army Air Forces base at Pendleton, Oregon, he had been flying training missions over the Pacific with the 34th Bomb Squadron of the 17th Bombardment Group. Griffin, age twenty-five, knew that the attack meant he soon would be flying combat missions instead.

Early in 1942, the Army Air Forces decided that the 17th Bombardment Group was particularly suited for a joint project it was planning with the Navy because the group flew the B-25, a small, twin-engine bomber that could fly farther than Navy fighters. In preparation for the joint venture, the group received orders on February 3 to move to Columbia Army Air Base in South Carolina. The 17th Bombardment Group's senior officers asked the airmen if they wanted to volunteer for a special mission. The catch? They had to decide without knowing any details about the mission—except that it was dangerous.

From Columbia, members of the group who had volunteered to participate went to Eglin Field, near the naval aviation base at Pensacola. At Eglin, the airmen met Lieutenant Colonel James Doolittle, who was helming the mission. Doolittle stressed the danger of the assignment and told the men that they could change their minds if they no longer wanted to volunteer. But he offered no additional details. The airmen didn't know that General Hap Arnold, commander of the Army Air Forces, had asked Doolittle to lead a team of airmen to fly from an aircraft carrier to bomb Japan itself. The team would consist of eighty airmen to participate in the mission as well as several others who could replace them if and however necessary.

The mission, if successful, would give Americans hope.

The mission's goal: to damage Japanese military and industrial facilities and to create psychological damage by shattering Japan's belief in its own invincibility. Just as important, the mission, if successful, would give Americans hope. It would show a nation demoralized by the devastating attack on Pearl Harbor that America could marshal its forces and deliver a powerful counterblow to its Pacific aggressor. In short, the mission would show that America and its allies could win the war.

Griffin didn't hesitate. He volunteered quickly. Nor did Doolittle and the 17th Bombardment Group's senior officers have any trouble finding volunteers. They had more than enough. They accepted Griffin's offer to join the team because they knew he was a good navigator.

After dropping their bombs, the planes would continue on long hauls to China, where they would land. At Eglin Field, the aircrews learned how to get a B-25 off the ground in 450 feet or fewer—an exceptionally short distance for a plane that usually needed 1,000 to 1,400 feet to take off under normal conditions. The airmen practiced simulated takeoffs, but they didn't have the chance to undertake even one trial takeoff from an aircraft carrier. As the aircrews trained, ground crews modified the B-25s to carry more fuel and made changes necessary for them to take off from a carrier.

In addition to his flying duties, Griffin received another assignment. He went to Washington, DC, with Captain David Jones, a pilot, to collect information about targets in Japan. But the two men were told in no uncertain terms to avoid one theoretically possible site: the Tokyo Imperial Palace. An unsuccessful attack on Emperor Hirohito would unite the Japanese, just as the attack on Pearl Harbor had united Americans. They couldn't risk it.

After a few weeks at Eglin Field, Griffin and the other airmen flew to McClellan Field in Sacramento, California, where ground crews installed new propellers and continued to work on the B-25s. The aircraft then flew to their final land-based destination, Alameda Naval Air Station on San Francisco Bay.

Doolittle welcomed the airmen as they arrived. He wanted to make sure every crewmember and every plane was ready to board the USS *Hornet*, the carrier chosen to transport the men and their B-25s. As Griffin boarded the *Hornet*, he made an observation: The runway looked awfully short.

With the *Hornet* ready to depart, Doolittle let the airmen spend the evening ashore. Griffin hit the Top of the Mark, a nightclub overlooking the bay. From there he could see the B-25s on the *Hornet*. As the men returned to the carrier that night, many still didn't know where it was taking them. Griffin knew because he had helped collect information on the targets. He also knew that the team assembled by Lieutenant Colonel Doolittle was about to embark on exactly the dangerous mission that Doolittle had promised.

Carrying sixteen B-25s and eighty airmen, plus extra crews, the *Hornet* sailed under the Golden Gate Bridge and into the Pacific on the morning of April 2, 1942. Seven escort ships accompanied it. In short order, Captain Marc Mitscher, the commanding officer, announced on

"Army pilots, man your planes!"

the carrier's PA system that they were sailing toward Tokyo. Doolittle gave the crews detailed information about their mission and targets. Now they understood the purpose of their training at Eglin Field.

★

ON APRIL 18, THE *HORNET* LAY 650 MILES FROM JAPAN, ABOUT 250 MILES short of the location where Doolittle wanted the planes to leave the carrier. But Captain Mitscher had received intelligence that Japanese vessels lay nearby. Those vessels easily could convey information about the carrier to Japan that would enable the Japanese navy to attack it. The aircrews had no choice but to depart earlier than planned.

At 8 a.m., Captain Mitscher spoke again into the PA system: "Army pilots, man your planes!"

Griffin was in the wardroom of the *Hornet* when he heard the announcement. He and other airmen were being briefed for their flights, which they expected to occur at a later time. But of course they didn't know that Japanese vessels were nearing the *Hornet*. Griffin raced to his plane, the *Whirling Dervish*. Doolittle flew the first B-25 off the carrier at 8:20 a.m. in the hopes that doing so would give his men the confidence to realize that they, too, could do the same.

The sea was rough, the sky cloudy, the winds strong. Sometimes the wind blew so hard that, as the planes took off, Griffin had to hold on to the rods on deck to which ropes were tied to secure the aircraft when parked there.

First Lieutenant Harold Watson, pilot of the *Whirling Dervish*, revved the engines. Sitting at the navigator's table, Griffin sublimated his emotions. He had to remain calm. The *Whirling Dervish* took off at 8:50 a.m., the ninth of sixteen planes to depart the *Hornet*.

To avoid detection by Japanese forces, the *Dervish* flew at an altitude of one hundred feet for much of the trip. During the flight, Griffin made his way from the navigator's table to the cockpit to talk with Watson and the copilot, Second Lieutenant James Parker. The crew spotted some Japanese planes, but none confronted them.

They devised a contingency plan in case the plane ran out of fuel either before or shortly after it dropped its payload on Tokyo: They would ditch the *Dervish* near a Japanese boat and try to commandeer it with their pistols.

The weather improved as the crew neared Tokyo. Only a few clouds floated in the sky. Their target was the Tokyo Gas and Electric Company, which lay in the southern part of the city. Griffin had studied the target when he had gone to Washington, DC.

Watson took the *Dervish* up to 1,500 feet. Sergeant Wayne Bissell, the bombardier, released the B-25's four bombs, striking the building. Watson pulled away and resumed flying at low altitude to avoid anti-aircraft fire. The *Dervish* flew over the imperial palace. As instructed, the crew refrained from attacking it.

The *Dervish* flew over the imperial palace.

Griffin felt calm. He and his crew had accomplished their mission. They had helped America. Because of them, the gas and electric company couldn't produce power for several days.

★

AFTER THE ATTACK, WATSON WANTED TO PUT JAPAN BEHIND THEM AS quickly as possible. He headed south to the Pacific, flying just a few yards above the waves. A Japanese cruiser fired flak at the plane, but all the shells missed. Flying through the spray rising from where the shells hit the water, the *Dervish* continued southward until it had gone far enough to turn west toward China.

The initial goal was to reach a Chinese airport about three hundred miles inland, but the B-25s had left the *Hornet* hundreds of miles sooner than planned. The crew suspected that their plane already had used the fuel they needed to go that far inland. Griffin feared that he and his crewmates wouldn't reach Chinese shores.

As the aircraft flew westward, Griffin noticed an unexpected ally: a tailwind. A strong, unanticipated wind pushed them toward China. They might not have to ditch in the Pacific after all.

But that wind blew them not only toward China but also toward a storm. Enveloped in clouds, fog, and rain, Griffin couldn't navigate toward an airport. He needed to see stars or landmarks. He could see neither. So Watson's flight plan was simple: Fly at ten thousand feet until the sputtering engines ran out of fuel. All of the crew were wearing their parachutes. Everyone except Watson, who remained in the pilot's seat, lined up and was ready to jump.

The sputtering started after the *Dervish* had been airborne for

The sputtering started after the *Dervish* had been airborne for fifteen and a half hours.

fifteen and a half hours. Griffin didn't know exactly where they were, but he guessed that they had gone far enough to be flying over Chinese territory not controlled by Japan. Watson gave the order. Griffin and his crewmates, followed by the pilot, leapt out of the plane and into the storm.

Severe winds collapsed Griffin's parachute. It reopened, collapsed, and opened again. As he descended, it lodged in the top of a bamboo tree. Caught on the tree, Griffin released his harness—only to find himself on a slick, muddy hillside. He held on to the tree to keep himself from sliding down and stayed awake all night.

In the morning, he walked into a valley, as did two of his crewmates: Parker, the copilot, and Technical Sergeant Eldred Scott, the engineer/gunner. The three men fired their pistols into the air to identify themselves as American fliers. According to protocol, an airman fired one shot, and a comrade who heard it responded with two. After converging, the three men walked through the countryside until they came across locals who helped them. They had landed a hundred miles south of Poyang Lake in southeast China—about three hundred miles inland.

The Chinese took Griffin, Parker, and Scott to meet two American Catholic priests, who identified the fliers as Americans who had attacked Japan. The Chinese regarded the three airmen as heroes and took them to the *Dervish* so they could collect any personal items that had survived the crash.

Soon Watson, the pilot, joined the trio. His shoulder had broken when he parachuted out, so he needed more assistance than his crewmates. Bissell, the bombardier, was the last of the crew to rejoin the group. He had parachuted out of the plane successfully, but bandits found him and held him for ransom in the hope of receiving money. He escaped, though, and met friendly locals who helped him.

The Chinese put the airmen up in houses and schools and helped the crew travel west to Hengyang, a city with an airport. An American plane flew the crew from Hengyang to Chungking, China's wartime capital. Griffin attended a luncheon held to honor the participants of the April 18 attack. They became known as Doolittle Raiders. General Chiang Kai-shek and Madame Chiang attended the lunch. Then Griffin and his crewmates flew back to America. He arrived home in Chicago in June to see his family again.

Several participants in the raid weren't so fortunate, however. Three airmen died when they bailed out or crash-landed. The Japanese captured eight men and executed three of them. Another died of malnutrition. The raid had angered and embarrassed Japan's military leaders. In retaliation, Japanese forces killed an estimated 250,000 Chinese.

★

WHILE ON LEAVE, GRIFFIN WENT TO A FRIEND'S COTTAGE IN MICHIGAN, where he met a young woman, Esther Jones. Knowing that the raiders

They became known as Doolittle Raiders.

An anti-aircraft shell struck the cockpit windshield and exploded.

---

had become famous, Miss Jones expected Griffin to act like a braggart. But she quickly realized that he was a modest gentleman. Griffin and Jones engaged to marry that summer.

After his leave, Griffin was promoted to captain. He went with the 438th Bomb Squadron of the 319th Bombardment Group to Maison Blanche Airfield in northern Algeria in November 1942. The squadron flew B-26 Marauders, twin-engine bombers. He knew his commanding officer quite well: James Doolittle, now a major general, was commanding the 12th Air Force in North Africa.

On January 23, 1943, Griffin was flying in a B-26 called *Hell's Cargo* on a patrol flight, heading east toward Sicily. His squadron's goal was to attack German supply ships in the Mediterranean. The sky that morning was bright blue.

The crew came across a German freighter, and the pilot, First Lieutenant Chuck Meyers, flew toward it. As *Hell's Cargo* approached, an anti-aircraft shell struck the cockpit windshield and exploded, striking both Meyers and the copilot, First Lieutenant Bennett Grimm. Blood covered their faces. Despite his injuries, though, Grimm released the bombs, which hit the freighter.

Meyers called Griffin, who had been in the nose of the aircraft firing a machine gun, to the cockpit. As Meyers flew them toward the Tunisian coast, Griffin gave first aid to the two men.

But one of the aircraft's engines stopped working. Then the second engine failed. Meyers had no choice but to ditch *Hell's Cargo* about half a mile from shore. All five crewmembers escaped through the hatches and dropped into the cold Mediterranean waters. With Meyers's help, Griffin pulled Grimm on a flotation cushion to the beach. As they drew close, two Arabs saw the men, came to help, and took them to a hut. Griffin went to seek assistance and found a Frenchman, who arranged for a British medical team to take the injured men to a field hospital.

Three months later, on the first anniversary of the raid on Japan, Doolittle brought together the participants of the raid who were serving in North Africa. Doolittle, Griffin, and the other airmen toasted their comrades with champagne.

★

IN JULY, THE ALLIES IN NORTH AFRICA WERE PREPARING TO LAUNCH Operation Husky, the invasion of Sicily. To weaken German forces in advance of the invasion, the 319th Bombardment Group sent thirty-nine B-26s to attack Sicilian airfields on July 4. Griffin's pilot that day was Captain Griffith Williams, who also had participated in the Tokyo raid, and flying with them was a special passenger: Lieutenant Colonel Wilbur Aring, the group commander.

Griffin wanted to take photos of Sicily during the flight, so he knew he might be moving around the plane. Before departing Djedeida Airfield in Tunisia, the group's base, Griffin stashed a parachute near his navigator's table as well as one in the rear of the aircraft. He also wore an unusual piece of equipment: a German helmet. He had found the helmet and thought it would provide better protection than his American helmet because it curved around his ears.

As he flew through the clear blue sky over Sicily, Griffin stood with a camera at one of the waist gunner's windows. But the beauty of the sky changed suddenly when German ground troops fired anti-aircraft shells, hitting the plane several times. Flames spewed from the left engine of the aircraft. Then German fighters appeared.

I've had it, Griffin thought.

He located the closest parachute, walked to the escape hatch, and sat on the edge. He was ready to leap out when he remembered that he was wearing the German helmet. He didn't want to be captured with it, so he put it down at the rear of the plane and went back to the hatch.

Group Commander Aring wasn't impressed. "Hurry up and get out of here!" he shouted.

Griffin's chute opened properly, but as he came down he noticed a German pilot in a Messerschmitt 109 flying toward him. It turned upward and looked like the pilot was trying to shoot him but couldn't because the guns had jammed. The pilot repeated this maneuver several times, but the Messerschmitt's guns never fired, and Griffin landed safely in a wheat field.

Soldiers in a German anti-aircraft crew who had seen him descending raced toward him. Speaking in English, Griffin told them that he wanted to talk to their commanding officer. The soldiers took him to see a general. Griffin informed the general that he wanted to

---

Flames spewed from the left engine of the aircraft. Then German fighters appeared.

"Herr Hauptmann, he was not trying to shoot you; he was taking your picture."

make a formal complaint about a German pilot trying to shoot him after he had bailed out.

"Herr Hauptmann," said the general, referring to Griffin's rank as a captain, "he was not trying to shoot you; he was taking your picture."

Griffin wisely dropped his complaint but refused to give any information other than his name, rank, and serial number.

"Take him away," the general said.

The Nazis took Griffin by train and truck to the Dulag Luft interrogation center near Frankfurt, Germany. Again, he gave only his name, rank, and serial number. From the interrogation center, they took him to Stalag Luft III, a Luftwaffe camp at Sagan, one hundred miles southeast of Berlin. At that time, the Luftwaffe hadn't yet built a separate compound for American airmen, so the Germans placed him in the camp's north compound with many British officers.

One of Griffin's fellow prisoners was Captain Williams, pilot of the B-26 on the flight to Sicily. Griffin and Williams boldly decided to dig an escape tunnel about fifteen feet under their barracks. The camp's guards discovered the tunnel, however, ending their attempt to escape.

After the Germans built the south compound for Americans and transferred Griffin to it, seventy-six men escaped from a tunnel carefully constructed at the north compound. The Germans recaptured all but three of those men and executed fifty of them. Years later, that escape inspired fellow prisoner Paul Brickhill to write his account of the breakout, *The Great Escape*, which later became the feature film starring Steve McQueen, James Garner, Richard Attenborough, Charles Bronson, and others.

Back in the south compound, Griffin was designated commanding officer of hut 103. His room in the hut held more than just a place to sleep, though. It contained an eighteen-inch cupboard hidden by a false wall. In the cupboard, he hid maps, identification forms that prisoners could use if they escaped, and other items. But the guards eventually discovered the cupboard and charged Griffin with destruction of Reich property. Griffin had a rather different perspective on the situation: He thought he was *improving* Reich property. Despite his protestations, camp staff sentenced him to time in solitary confinement.

The discovery of the hidden cupboard was a temporary setback, but Griffin viewed other problems that arose in the hut more seriously. Some airmen from southern states mistreated a fellow POW who had flown with the Tuskegee Airmen. Griffin warned the white officers that he would report their conduct to the Army Air Forces after the war if they didn't change their tune. His position was clear: All Americans should be treated equally, regardless of the color of their skin. The problem resolved itself when northern airmen heard about the situation and invited the black officer to move in with them.

★

GRIFFIN'S TIME AT STALAG LUFT III CAME TO AN ABRUPT END ON JANUARY 27, 1945. The Germans ordered him and the other prisoners to depart the camp immediately. They could take only what they could carry.

Ironically, Griffin heard the news while watching the Pulitzer Prize–winning George S. Kaufman and Moss Hart play *You Can't Take It with You*. He had just enough time to grab gloves and woolen socks.

The Nazi government was relocating the prisoners because it feared that Soviet forces, advancing from the east, could take control of the camp. The Germans hoped to use the prisoners to negotiate more favorable terms in a peace agreement with the Allies. If the POWs came under Allied control, the Germans had nothing of value with which to negotiate.

About 2,500 men from the compound marched into the cold winter night, and they kept marching through the German countryside for the next two and a half days. The guards put the men in boxcars and moved them by train to Stalag VII-A, a massive, overcrowded camp near Moosburg in southern Bavaria.

Two American tanks and a command car from General George Patton's Third Army arrived at the camp's main gate on April 29, 1945.

Tom Griffin was free.

But the Army still had a war to fight and wasn't prepared to feed so many former prisoners. In response, Griffin and other former prisoners walked to nearby farmhouses, knocked on the doors, and said, "Essen, bitte." Food, please.

The farmers invited them in and fed them.

★

Tom Griffin was free.

Tom Griffin in 2012.

GRIFFIN SOON FLEW TO CAMP LUCKY STRIKE, AN AMERICAN BASE NEAR LE Havre, France. Well fed there, he boarded a ship bound for New York City. Rising majestically from New York Harbor, the Statue of Liberty greeted him, symbolizing in one emotional moment everything for which he had fought.

In New York, Griffin boarded a train to Chicago to reunite with his family once more and to start a new one with Esther Jones. He left the Army Air Forces and began a new career as an accountant in Cincinnati. Shortly before he died in 2013 at the age of ninety-six, Griffin said he was surprised that people treated the participants in the Tokyo attack as celebrities in the postwar era. He enjoyed talking to people who knew he had been a Doolittle Raider, but as Griffin put it, "We were simply fighting a war for our side."

He never did discover what the German pilot did with the photos taken of him as he parachuted over Sicily.

★ ★ ★

THE FLYING FORTRESS

RALPH BURBRIDGE
Second Lieutenant
414th Squadron
97th Bomb Group
US Army Air Forces

A S PART OF AN ALLIED CAMPAIGN TO DRIVE GERMAN FORCES from North Africa, about fifty bombers departed from Biskra Airfield in northern Algeria on February 1, 1943. The *All American*, a B-17 Flying Fortress, dodged enemy fire from Messerschmitt 109 fighters as it approached the harbor in Bizerte, Tunisia, but the Nazi fighters didn't damage the aircraft. Second Lieutenant Ralph Burbridge, the bombardier, released the B-17's 500-pound bombs on the harbor, fulfilling the ship's mission.

More Messerschmitt 109s attacked as the *All American* turned to head back to base, but again they inflicted no damage on the Flying Fortress.

First Lieutenant Kendrick Bragg, the pilot, and his crew hoped that the rest of the flight would prove uneventful. Bragg had played with Duke University's football team in the 1939 Rose Bowl and chose the name *All American* for the aircraft to honor his diverse crew. Regardless of whether their families came from England, Greece, Italy, or elsewhere, they were "all American."

Sitting on a stool in the nose of the bomber, Burbridge spotted two 109 fighters about two miles away. They were flying at about 10,000 feet on the right side of the bomber. Suddenly they turned around. One raced toward the *All American*, flames leaping from the guns on its wings. The other attacked another B-17.

Burbridge fired a .30-caliber machine gun at the attacking 109. At the same time, the navigator, First Lieutenant Harry Nuessle, also in the nose, fired at the other Messerschmitt.

The fighter flying toward the *All American* rolled over on its left side. Presumably, the pilot intended to complete the roll and fly under the bomber. The shells Burbridge fired might have hit the German pilot or damaged his plane—or both. But the fighter never completed its roll. Instead, it continued flying directly toward them at 350 miles an hour.

As the seconds slid by, the 109 flew closer and closer. The fighter was moments away from striking the bomber, moments away from killing everyone aboard both planes. Panic raced through Burbridge. Despite his fear, he kept firing—and the 109 kept coming. Then the Messerschmitt crashed through the upper middle section of the *All American.*

The German plane instantly broke apart. The B-17 tilted upward, then down, but Bragg kept the aircraft stable. The collision jolted Burbridge less than expected: After all, the 109 was much smaller and lighter than a Flying Fortress. It was like a motorcycle running into a bus. Burbridge remained seated on his stool during the collision.

The *All American* crew had survived, and the bomber was still flying, but no one knew whether it could make it all the way back to Biskra Airfield—roughly three hundred miles away. The crew surveyed the damage: The Messerschmitt's wing had opened a gap, two feet wide, from the middle of the upper fuselage down to the tail. The 109 had split the bomber almost in half. It also had sheared off the left tail wing completely. The damage had rendered the fuselage so weak that the tail section was wobbling. The *All American* looked doomed.

Nuessle, the navigator, intercommed Bragg, who relayed the

The Messerschmitt's wing had opened a gap, two feet wide, from the middle of the upper fuselage down to the tail.

Charles Cutforth took what became a famous photo of the *All American*.

dreadful information that the crew at the rear had given him: There was a "hole in the side of the ship big enough for a jeep to ride through."

Burbridge donned his parachute in case the plane went down. But despite the damage, Bragg told the crew he was going to try to fly back to Biskra.

Other Allied bombers from the Bizerte raid slowed down to protect the *All American*. American fighters also flew overhead. This escort service raised the beleaguered crew's spirits.

Flying nearby was another B-17, the *Flying Flit Gun*. Lieutenant Charles "Cliff" Cutforth, navigator on the *Flit Gun*, spotted the damage. That a plane could fly in that condition amazed him. He had a camera with him and snapped a photo of the *All American*.

Once the convoy had flown beyond the range of the German fighters, the escort planes resumed full speed and departed. There was nothing more they could do to help.

★

The ground crew feared the worst.

RALPH BURBRIDGE GREW UP IN THE TOWN OF LOUISIANA, MISSOURI, AND joined the Army Air Corps, the predecessor of the Army Air Forces, in 1940. The Japanese attack on Pearl Harbor the following year shocked and angered him and, like so many others, prompted him to action. He was twenty-one years old at the time.

Serving with the 414th Squadron of the 97th Bomb Group, Burbridge flew combat missions from England before his squadron moved to North Africa. He had flown in the first major American raid on German-controlled territory, but he had never flown in a plane as badly damaged as the *All American.*

★

WHEN THE *ALL AMERICAN* DIDN'T ARRIVE AT BISKRA AIRFIELD WITH THE other American planes, the ground crew feared the worst.

Burbridge, however, felt quite safe. If the crew could survive a dead-on collision with a 109, they could survive anything. He had confidence in Bragg and faith in their rugged B-17, now flying all on its own.

The short return trip felt like it was taking years, but minute by minute the bomber came closer to its base. An hour and forty-five minutes after the attack, the *All American* approached Biskra. The crew fired a flare to indicate that they needed to make an emergency landing.

The ground crew immediately dispatched an ambulance to the end of the runway.

Gradually, the plane descended. The front wheels came down properly, but the rear wheel didn't. The plane skidded the last hundred yards on the runway before coming to a final, marvelous stop.

Bragg spotted the ambulance. "No business, Doc!" he shouted through a cockpit window, meaning: No one was injured. Everyone was safe. Several members of the ground crew climbed onto the fuselage of the *All American* to inspect the damage, and the rear section collapsed. Burbridge and the rest of the flight crew were happy to be alive.

Burbridge learned that Cutforth had taken a photo of his plane, which surprised and pleased him. Without that shot, he doubted that anyone would believe a plane could fly in such a condition. Burbridge had no idea, however, that he and the crew were about to become legends. He was just doing his job.

The story of the Flying Fortress that wouldn't stop flying spread about as fast as the Messerschmitt had been flying toward the *All American*. It fired the country's imagination. Boeing, which made B-17s, used Lieutenant Cutforth's photo for an ad in *Life* magazine boasting how sturdy its aircraft were. The ad noted coolly that theoretically, under those circumstances, the plane shouldn't have been able to fly.

The commander of the 97th Bomb Group gave the crew a few days of leave. They flew to Egypt to see Cairo, Alexandria, and the

He and the crew were about to become legends.

pyramids at Giza. Afterward, the crew of the *All American* resumed flying in other aircraft.

After completing fifty-two missions, Burbridge returned to the United States in July 1943 to train bombardiers. The residents of Louisiana, Missouri, hailed him as a war hero and held a parade as well as banquets to honor him. Later, he studied journalism and business at the University of Missouri. After graduation, he worked for the *Herald-Whig*, a newspaper in Quincy, Illinois. Later,

In 2012, Ralph Burbridge holds a note of appreciation from his former squadron for his wartime service.

he worked for the Easter Seal Society and with disabled veterans. Ralph Burbridge died at his home in Des Moines, Washington, in 2013 at the age of ninety-two.

When asked about the message or moral of his famous flight, he simply said: "You don't give up."

WHITE CLIFFS

ROBERT PATTERSON
Second Lieutenant
336th Squadron
95th Bomb Group
US Army Air Forces

H E KNEW THE ATTACK ON PEARL HARBOR WOULD UNITE AND galvanize Americans. Deeply angered like so many, Robert Patterson, a twenty-year-old student at Lafayette College in Easton, Pennsylvania, immediately decided to leave college. He wanted to fight. He had developed an interest in planes as a teenager, and now he would do whatever it took to join the war—even if that meant going to Canada to enlist in the Royal Canadian Air Force.

Despite Patterson's noble intentions, however, the US Army Air Forces (AAF) initially didn't accept him. At Mitchel Field on Long Island, Patterson learned that his eyesight wasn't good enough—but he didn't lose sight of his goal. Determined, Patterson visited an optometrist in his hometown of Freeport, New York, who prescribed exercises and corrective glasses. Patterson's eyesight improved significantly.

When he tried to enlist again, Patterson discovered that he had another problem. His heart beat too fast. So he sought out a chiropractor, who helped him lower his pulse to an acceptable level.

The AAF duly accepted Patterson, but they needed bomber crews more than fighter pilots, so they trained him to fly B-17 Flying Fortress bombers.

★

SECOND LIEUTENANT BOB PATTERSON WAS POSTED TO AN AIR BASE AT Horham in Suffolk, England, as a copilot with the 336th Squadron of the 95th Bomb Group. On July 30, 1943, he; the pilot, First Lieutenant Bob Jutzi; and the rest of the crew were preparing to embark on a raid over Kassel in central Germany. As the crew boarded their aircraft,

The explosions sounded like thunder.

they discovered it had mechanical problems and wouldn't be ready to fly in time for the mission, so they switched to another aircraft and then took off.

As they approached Belgium, the crew saw flak. Within minutes, three shells hit their aircraft. One ripped a large hole in the tail, another struck the nose, and the third hit three of the four engines. The explosions sounded like thunder. Smoke flew from the inner left engine. The shells also damaged the instrument panel and Patterson's oxygen supply. He quickly located a spare bottle of oxygen and added it to his system. Jutzi and Patterson knew they had to turn the aircraft around, but they doubted it could fly back to England on only one engine. Patterson was scared.

About twenty minutes after the flak hit the plane, he intercommed the crew: "Stand by to bail out." But because of the noise, some of the crew didn't hear the command clearly. They heard "bail out" but not "stand by." Mistakenly thinking they were following orders, five members of the crew bailed out. Bob Randall, a radio operator, died after he bailed. His body washed up at Flushing on the south coast of England.

Jutzi and Patterson, both wearing their life jackets, sent a distress signal in the hope that someone would hear it. The fuselage wasn't on fire, so they decided not to order the remaining members of the crew to bail but chose instead to ditch the plane in the Channel. To slow the B-17, they lowered the flaps and turned the top-turret guns forward, the

With the help of British rescue crews, they might survive.

increased wind resistance slowing the plane. Lieutenant Wilbur Collins, the bombardier, and Lieutenant Ralph Guinzburg, the navigator, threw equipment from the bomber to make it lighter. The other member of the crew still on board was Technical Sergeant Harry Knotts, the engineer/top-turret gunner.

As the aircraft descended, Patterson saw the white cliffs of Dover just a few miles away. They were close to England—which meant, with the help of British rescue crews, they might survive.

With scant minutes to go before their water landing, Jutzi and Patterson tightened their seat belts. Collins, Guinzburg, and Knotts sat nervously in the radio room. All five men braced themselves for a rough landing, but the aircraft landed smoothly on the calm channel. The water, however, splashed up to the cockpit windshield and rushed into the radio room, tossing the men roughly around. Jutzi and Patterson escaped from the cockpit through a window on the right side that they lifted up and pushed out. Neither sustained any injuries.

Guinzburg wasn't so lucky: He was bleeding from cuts above one of his eyes. Collins released two yellow life rafts from their compartments in the fuselage just behind the upper turret. Carbon dioxide cylinders automatically inflated the rafts—but not all the men could get into them. Knotts, injured by the rushing water, found himself trapped on the radio room floor. Jutzi, Guinzburg, and Collins helped him. Guinzburg went underwater to push him from below while Jutzi and Collins pulled from above. The three men quickly freed Knotts and helped him out of the plane. Then the five men climbed into the rubber rafts. Within minutes, the nose of the aircraft started slipping into the English Channel, and the entire plane sank.

Robert Patterson in uniform for his ninety-second birthday in 2013.

Shortly thereafter, two British Spitfires flew toward the rafts. The pilots waggled their wings so the men in the rafts knew they weren't alone. The Spitfires were launching a rescue mission. One of the Spitfires remained near the rafts, circling them. The other flew off and returned with a British Supermarine Walrus amphibious biplane. The pilot of the Spitfire accompanying the Walrus dropped a smoke flare near the rafts so the Walrus pilot knew exactly where to land. When the Walrus landed, Patterson and his four crewmates had been in the water for about twenty minutes that seemed like an eternity. The airmen climbed into the Walrus just as two speedboats also arrived to rescue them. The Walrus pilot declared the five men his "booty" and wanted to fly them to Dover.

But the Walrus didn't have enough power to fly with five passengers, so the pilot taxied the plane to Dover. An ambulance at the Dover naval base took the men to a hospital, where a surgeon treated Guinzburg and Knotts for head injuries. After hot baths, warm food, fresh clothes, and some scotch, everyone except Guinzburg flew back to Horham in a B-17. Guinzburg remained in the hospital for additional medical care.

★

PATTERSON SUCCESSFULLY COMPLETED TWENTY-FIVE COMBAT FLIGHTS and before reassignment to a transport group. After the war, he worked as a sales representative for a toy company. He now lives in Centerville on Cape Cod, Massachusetts.

A LONG WAY TO BRADENTON

JAMES ARMSTRONG
Second Lieutenant
546th Bomb Squadron
384th Bomb Group
US Army Air Forces

A RADIO IN HARRISON HALL ANNOUNCED THAT THE JAPANESE had attacked Pearl Harbor. James Armstrong—a native of Bradenton, Florida, who was studying civil engineering at Georgia Tech in Atlanta—couldn't understand how the attack could have occurred. But he knew it had changed his life. He completed his semester and, at age nineteen, joined the Army Air Forces in January 1942.

★

CONTRARY TO THE WEATHER REPORT FOR THE DAY, THE CLOUDS RAN thick on September 6, 1943.

Second Lieutenant James Armstrong was flying above Stuttgart, in southern Germany, and what he saw worried him. Now a B-17 pilot, Armstrong kept his eyes trained on the lead aircraft ahead of him to see when it dropped its payload on the target: the VKF ball-bearing plant. As soon as the lead aircraft released its bombs, Armstrong's bombardier, Second Lieutenant Wilbert Yee, would do the same. The lead aircraft, however, kept flying over Stuttgart and didn't drop anything.

At 24,000 feet, the crew on the lead bomber couldn't tell whether they were flying over the ball-bearing plant. The lead plane circled again and again, as did Armstrong's B-17, the *Yankee Raider*. Armstrong was growing anxious because every minute that he spent above Stuttgart

---

The crew on the lead bomber couldn't tell whether they were flying over the ball-bearing plant.

---

used fuel that he needed to fly back to his base at Grafton Underwood in the Midlands of England.

At last the lead aircraft dropped its bombs. Yee flicked the toggle switch to release *Yankee Raider*'s 500-pound bombs, and Armstrong turned back to base. A strong tailwind had pushed *Yankee Raider* toward Stuttgart, but that same wind now slowed the aircraft.

Soon the right inner engine started shaking. Then it lost power, reducing the aircraft's speed. Armstrong couldn't keep pace with the other B-17s from his squadron. As the others flew ahead, his plane was alone and vulnerable.

Then it happened. A German ground crew fired a flak shell that exploded close to *Yankee Raider*, piercing one of the aircraft's fuel tanks. Second Lieutenant Robert Stoner, the copilot, saw fuel spilling from the tank.

"Jim, we're losing a lot of gas!" Stoner said.

Second Lieutenant Creighton Carlin, the navigator, overheard Stoner's announcement. "Jim, let's go to Switzerland," Carlin suggested. On the horizon, about seventy-five miles away, Carlin could see the snow-covered peaks of that neutral country.

But Armstrong kept flying west. He thought they had enough fuel to reach the English Channel, where he could ditch the aircraft, but a quick observation by Staff Sergeant Clifford Hammock, the tail gunner, forced Armstrong to alter his route.

"Fighter! Six o'clock high!" Hammock shouted.

"Fighter! Six o'clock high!" Hammock shouted.

A German fighter plane was about to attack them from behind.

Armstrong immediately descended into clouds, hoping that the fighter pilot wouldn't be able to see the B-17. But the fighter followed *Yankee Raider* and fired. A bullet struck a piece of aluminum on the left wing, making it flap in the air.

The radio operator, Technical Sergeant Walter House, reported that Sergeant Olen Grant, a waist gunner, had been hit. A shell had exploded, striking Grant's right eye and cheekbone. House didn't know Grant's condition, but the gunner wasn't moving.

Then Yee, the bombardier, made an announcement that surprised Armstrong: "Carlin—he's gone!"

"*What?*" Armstrong said over the intercom.

Carlin had bailed out without waiting for the pilot to order the crew to abandon the aircraft. The news shocked Armstrong, but it also convinced him that everyone should get ready to leave.

"Get your chutes on!" he ordered.

Staff Sergeant James Redwing, the ball turret gunner, left his turret. Seeing Grant and his injuries, Redwing tried to help by pulling him toward a door and putting a parachute on him—but Redwing couldn't move his injured comrade.

Grant, injured but alive, urged Redwing to leave the plane. "You go on!" he said.

Redwing made his way to the side door. A bullet struck his head, and Redwing's body tumbled from the plane.

Another bullet struck *Yankee Raider*. This one landed behind Armstrong's seat and set the interior of the plane on fire.

"*Bail out!*" the pilot shouted.

"Bail out!"

All remaining members of the crew bailed except Grant, who was so badly injured that he couldn't leave the aircraft.

The fire near the cockpit burned Armstrong's hands and face. Smoke billowed so thickly that he had to close his eyes. Unable to see and fearing that the aircraft would explode, he didn't think he could help anyone still on the plane. His feet found the escape hatch on the floor, and Armstrong slipped through it.

He quickly pulled the ripcord, opening his parachute. As he descended, a Focke-Wulf 190 circled him, but the German fighter didn't attack him. Armstrong landed in a plowed field in northern France, which German forces had occupied. To help him find his way back to England, he had a sheet of French phrases, a map, and compass. He also had an escape kit.

Pilotless, *Yankee Raider* made a miraculously perfect landing on a sugar beet field near Etrépagny, in eastern Normandy. The bomber came to a halt across the street from an airport used by the Nazis. Despite his injuries, Grant staggered out of *Yankee Raider* and into an ambulance. German soldiers took him to a hospital in Paris and then, two months later, to a prison camp in Austria.

★

ARMSTRONG HIT THE GROUND HARDER THAN EXPECTED. AS HE REMOVED his parachute and started to walk toward the woods, he realized that he had injured his right ankle. He didn't bother to hide the parachute because the German pilot who had circled him would report the position where he landed.

Armstrong walked past a marsh and headed for a wooded area that he had spotted while descending. Approaching the woods, he saw a rough briar patch, which would provide sufficient cover to prevent German troops from seeing him. He stayed in the briar overnight.

When the sun rose, Armstrong left the briar patch, but his ankle hurt so much that he could take only small steps. Step by painful step, he made his way toward a field. He crossed it and came upon a concrete tunnel in a hillside that appeared to store farm equipment. He considered hiding in it, but German troops surely would search it. If they found him, he would have no way to escape.

He continued walking and soon came to a two-story house. Not sure how the occupants would respond to an American airman seeking help, he refrained from knocking on the door.

Instead, he returned to the briar. On the way, he came across a shallow stream. He lowered a rubber bag into it and dropped in a couple of purification tablets. As he was waiting for the tablets to sanitize the water, an old Frenchman sporting a black beret approached him.

Armstrong quickly pulled the phrase sheet from his pocket to explain his identity.

"*Aviateur Américain*," he said. (I'm an) American aviator.

The Frenchman pointed to the woods. "*Allez! Allez! Allez!*" Go, go, go!

Armstrong hobbled back into the woods.

Gaston Viguier was pleased to help. The old man, a veteran of the Great War, lived in a nearby house and soon returned to the woods with a pan of beef stew and vegetables. Armstrong hadn't eaten since he left his base in England, so he devoured the meal with gratitude.

Armstrong took out his silk escape map, and Viguier indicated that he was near the village of Gamaches-en-Vexin, halfway between Rouen and Paris. In the woods, Armstrong had spent a lot of time studying his map, trying to decide the best way to leave France. Rouen lay to the northwest, closer to England; Paris to the southeast, farther from England but home to many members of the Resistance. Armstrong needed help from the Resistance if he was going to escape.

Viguier continued taking food to Armstrong for a few days, but his wife grew concerned about the risk he was taking. German troops usually treated Allied prisoners with military respect, but not so the French civilians who assisted the Allies. No, the Nazis shot them outright.

Eight days after Armstrong had parachuted into France, Viguier told him that he had to leave. Nazi troops were combing the area for escaped airmen. Armstrong pulled out his silk map again and asked for directions to Paris. The old man led Armstrong to a bridge and pointed toward Paris. The French veteran and the American airman shook hands.

"*Merci beaucoup*," Armstrong said in his southern accent.

★

Nazi troops were combing the area for escaped airmen.

STONER, THE COPILOT, HAD BAILED BEFORE ARMSTRONG AND HAD watched the pilot come down to earth, landing on a nearby hill. After hiding his parachute in some bushes, Stoner ran to the hill to meet Armstrong. Stoner couldn't find Armstrong, but he did find his chute, which he gathered and hid with his own.

Alfred Mourette, another French veteran of World War I, saw Stoner and hid him and two other members of the crew in a shed. Mourette asked whether he could have the two parachutes because women used the nylon chutes during the war to make lingerie. Stoner smiled and gladly handed them over.

★

ON SEPTEMBER 15, THE DAY AFTER ARMSTRONG SET OUT FOR PARIS, LAURA Armstrong, his mother, received a telegram from the War Department indicating that her son had been missing in action since September 6. Mrs. Armstrong twinged with alarm. When her husband returned home from the naval base at Port Everglades, he pointed out that the telegram said "missing in action." There was still a chance their son was alive.

In France, Armstrong often thought about his mother. With his father working some two hundred miles away, she was on her own at their home on Sixteenth Avenue West in Bradenton. This was the same home that he had buzzed for amusement while learning to fly a B-17 at Hendricks Field in central Florida, about sixty miles away. Fortunately for his military career, no one had reported a low-flying plane above his hometown that day. As Armstrong made his way toward Paris, he thought about what a long way it was to Bradenton.

★

ARMSTRONG'S MAP DIDN'T INCLUDE THE COUNTRY ROADS IN EASTERN Normandy, but it did show the Seine, which flows northwest through Paris and Rouen toward Le Havre. He knew he would come across the river if he just kept walking southeast.

By now the pain in his ankle was abating, and the burns on his face and left hand were healing. His right hand, however, wasn't healing well. He still wore his flight jacket, but he had removed his name tag and the insignia showing his rank as a second lieutenant. He needed to be as inconspicuous as possible.

Just before the sun sank into the west on his first day of walking, Armstrong spotted a white house and a boy and a girl running beside it. He approached them with his phrase sheet. They called for a woman in the house—no doubt their mother.

The woman took the pilot into her dining room and gave him bread and water but then abruptly shouted, "*Allez!*" Armstrong asked whether he could sleep in the pasture at the back of the property. The woman agreed, but Armstrong left early the next morning in case fear overtook her and she reported him to the Germans.

After walking all day, Armstrong came across a lone farmhouse. A man was working in a shed beside it.

"*Bonjour, monsieur,*" Armstrong said, with phrase sheet in hand.

The man, a Russian émigré, delighted at meeting an American flier. He was so pleased that he started dancing and called for his ninety-year-old mother to come out of their house. The man asked his mother to bring something for the "*aviateur Américain.*" She brought a bundle of civilian clothes, including a white shirt, pants, and a black coat.

Armstrong changed into the civilian clothes, leaving the rest of his uniform there except for his shoes, which he kept. He also held on to his identification tag and compass.

The kind Russian gave him a bag of apples, bread, and butter, and, now looking like a Frenchman, Armstrong continued on his journey. After an hour, he spotted the Seine and the town of Vaux-sur-Seine. In an otherwise empty café, he showed the barmaid his phrase sheet. She immediately started screaming and ran out of the café and into the arms of a man passing by.

Armstrong showed the phrase sheet to the man, who understood that Armstrong was an Allied airman, but the passerby made hand motions advising the *"aviateur Américain"* to leave. Armstrong complied, relieved to end his fraught encounter with the barmaid.

The Seine flowed nearby, and Armstrong used it to guide him toward Paris. Soon he came across an apple orchard where a young couple were having a picnic. Again, he took out his phrase sheet. The couple offered him some of their wine, and he gave them some of the bread he had received earlier in the day to see if they would help him. But the couple quickly left, and Armstrong found a place to sleep in the orchard.

★

IN THE MORNING, THE SUN SHONE BRIGHTLY. THE PILOT SET OFF, HOPING that the pleasant weather offered a good omen for the day ahead. After an hour, he came across a house on a well-kept property near the village of Triel-sur-Seine. A young woman was peeling potatoes at a table between the house and an outbuilding. Once again he took out his phrase sheet, but she stood up and walked into the house.

Moments later, a well-dressed woman emerged, eyeing him and his phrase sheet. Raymonde Laurent lived with her husband, Alexandre, and son, Philippe. She spoke some English and believed Armstrong to be, as the phrase sheet said, *un aviateur Américain*. She invited him into her house and made him a meal of potatoes, eggs, bread, and milk. More important than the food, though, she knew a woman who spoke English well. Madame Laurent asked Annie Price to come to her home to speak to the roving airman.

Madame Price came as invited. Tall and slim, she suggested that they go to her home, about a quarter of a mile away, where they could talk more easily. She had been born in Brighton, England, married a Frenchman, and raised three children, but she and her husband had divorced. Armstrong found relief in being able to speak English again.

Madame Price arranged for another English speaker to listen to him as well. Edward Cotterell, an Englishman who worked with a shipping company in Paris before the war, came to see him that evening—along with three armed men. All four men belonged to the French Resistance. Cotterell's assignment was to interrogate Armstrong to ensure that he really was an American flier and not a German agent trying to infiltrate the Resistance. The three armed Resistance fighters had a separate assignment: execute Armstrong if Cotterell concluded that he wasn't an airman. Thankfully Armstrong's southern accent helped him pass the test, and the four men left, satisfied that Armstrong was who he said he was.

Madame Price made up a bed for Armstrong. After sleeping on the ground for more than a week, he relished the comfort of the mattress and the clean sheets. Price also gave him a razor, and he shaved for the first time since he had left England.

The next day, September 18, a Frenchman came to Price's home. He brought bandages for Armstrong's wounds and treated them. He also brought a gray suit, a white shirt, and a red tie. The plan: take Armstrong to Paris by train the following day.

Armstrong worried when Madame Price later told him about the train trip. He had been flying solo since parachuting out of *Yankee Raider*, and it had served him well so far. He wasn't used to traveling with others nor having to keep a close eye out for German troops searching for wandering airmen.

The Frenchman who brought the bandages didn't identify himself, but Alec Prochiantz, a thirty-year-old medical intern, also belonged to the Resistance. Cotterell had asked him to escort Armstrong to Paris.

On the afternoon of Sunday, September 19, the two men walked to the village's train station. Prochiantz gave Armstrong a train ticket and chatted with a married couple at the station, Jacques and Yvonne Peyron. Yvonne, Cotterell's daughter, lived in the same apartment complex as Prochiantz.

Wearing the suit, shirt, and tie that Prochiantz had given him, Armstrong boarded the train, along with his guide and the Peyrons. The train arrived at Gare Saint-Lazare in Paris without incident. No German troops or Gestapo agents confronted anyone.

After leaving the station, Armstrong caught sight of the Eiffel Tower, but, dressed in the suit and tie, he didn't feel like a tourist. He walked three miles south to Prochiantz's apartment on the Rue du Bac without attracting the attention of anyone who might want to check his identity. Armstrong didn't know it yet, but Jacques and Yvonne Peyron were helping him avoid being questioned. The couple walked ahead to speak

The French Resistance didn't trust Armstrong—not completely, not yet.

to police officers on the route, diverting their attention as Armstrong and Prochiantz walked by.

Armstrong relaxed, finally feeling safe again, when he entered Prochiantz's apartment. He trusted his unnamed escort. The French Resistance, however, didn't trust Armstrong—not completely, not yet. The Resistance was having difficulty confirming what Armstrong said about his flight to Stuttgart on September 6. The confusion arose because *Yankee Raider* had been a last-minute replacement for another aircraft. Armstrong knew nothing about this confusion, but Prochiantz subsequently confirmed Armstrong's story and saved his life.

The medical intern offered the pilot meat, bread, eggs, and fresh vegetables. He also continued treating the burns on Armstrong's hands and face.

★

AFTER A FEW DAYS, MAURICE COTTEREAU, ANOTHER MEMBER OF THE Resistance, arrived at Prochiantz's apartment in a wood-burning truck with a friend. They had come to take Armstrong to another hiding place, a café in Drancy, a suburb to the northeast of Paris. Cottereau worked in the café bar. After Cottereau offered Armstrong a glass of cognac, the friend pulled out a gun and showed Armstrong the ration coupons they had obtained by robbing government offices. Clearly they were willing to use force against the Germans—and anyone else—if necessary.

Armstrong shared a bedroom above the bar with Cottereau, who lived with a female friend. The aviator didn't like the lack of privacy, though, and wanted to move out. He did so after meeting Théodorine Quénot and two Allied airmen whom she was protecting, Staff Sergeant Floyd Terry, an American from Dallas, and Sergeant Vic Matthews, an Englishman from Maidestone in Kent. Madame Quénot offered Armstrong a spare room in her small stucco house on the Rue Alcide Vellard in the suburb of Bobigny. Armstrong had great respect for Madame Quénot, who was about fifty years old and had a twenty-one-year-old son. She had taken an enormous risk in sheltering the airmen, which could result in imprisonment, torture, or even death.

After a few days, another American airman, Second Lieutenant Andrew Lindsay from Monmouth, Maine, joined them. Lindsay had studied French in high school and college. His arrival dramatically helped the other airmen because now they had someone who could act as an interpreter between them and Madame Quénot.

The four airmen called their hostess "Queenie" and named their new home Queenie's Boarding House, of which the dining room became the focal point. They used it not only for meals but also to play cards and to listen to newscasts on the BBC's international service. From the news-casts, they plotted on a map the cities that Russian troops had recap-tured from the Nazis. Each day, the men hoped to hear that the Soviets were close or that the Western Allies had launched their long-awaited invasion of France.

Madame Quénot showed great patience with the airmen. Although she slept on a bed in the dining room, she didn't object if the men stayed up late to listen to newscasts on the radio.

The airmen also ate relatively well. They had a good supply of bread, eggs, and meat. The Resistance happily used stolen ration coupons and the black market to feed Allied airmen who had risked their lives in the effort to liberate France.

A few days after Armstrong arrived at her home, Madame Quénot walked with him and Terry to the café where he had stayed previously. From there, Cottereau, the bartender, took the two airmen to a studio to have their photos taken for false identification cards. On the way back, they passed a three-story building surrounded by barbed wire on Rue Arthur Fontaine. Armstrong asked about it. In broken English, Cottereau revealed it to be a prison that held three thousand Jews.

Armstrong wondered why so many Jews were in one place. Like so many other Allied servicemen in 1943, he hadn't known of such camps or that the Nazis were gathering and murdering Jews. Armstrong may not have known what was happening within the prison's walls, but in those walls he saw one of the many reasons that America was fighting the Third Reich. The prison was the Drancy transit camp, originally designed as a housing complex. After France fell in 1940, French police detained arrested Jews there. Trains later transported them to concentration camps in German territory. Few survived.

★

IN OCTOBER, THE ALLIED GUESTS BEGAN LEAVING QUEENIE'S BOARDING House. First, Matthews and Lindsay departed. Armstrong didn't know where they were going—probably taking a long journey back to England.

Armstrong and Terry missed their comrades, but a few days later they also departed. One evening, Madame Quénot walked with them to Cottereau's café in Drancy. They, too, didn't know their final destination. They had no choice but to trust the members of the Resistance who were helping them.

Armstrong now carried a false ID card containing the photo of him taken the previous month. To anyone who stopped him, he wasn't Second Lieutenant James Armstrong, an American born on August 3, 1922; now he was Jean Riber, a Frenchman born on January 16, 1920. The card identified him as a *charcutier*, or pork butcher.

At the café, six American airmen were waiting for them. Armstrong knew one of them: Second Lieutenant John Heald, an American who had served as bombardier on one of his crews.

After some cognac, Armstrong and Terry thanked Madame Quénot for her help and then boarded a truck that took them and the other six airmen to a Métro station. There Armstrong and Terry were assigned to a man aged about forty, who served as their escort. The three men took the Métro to a rail station where they caught a train to Quimper, a city in Brittany. Their guide chatted to Armstrong and Terry in French, even though the two men couldn't understand a word. He wanted any German agents watching to think they were three Frenchmen on a routine train trip—not two American airmen and a member of the Resistance.

After the train departed, their guide walked up the aisle of their coach to look for a suitable compartment for the two men. He found one in which several elderly people were sitting. Armstrong and Terry joined them. To avoid conversation, the two men pretended to sleep. Armstrong feared that the other passengers might suspect him and

Terry of being Allied soldiers if they discovered that the two men couldn't speak French.

The train rolled toward Quimper all night, stopping at several stations along the way. At 11 a.m. the next day, it pulled into its final destination. In the bright but crisp daylight, all eight airmen disembarked into an attractive town built around the Odet River. But they didn't have their eyes on the river; they had spotted German soldiers in green uniforms. The men pretended to be tourists and followed their guides to a church. Thankfully the Nazi soldiers didn't question Armstrong or his fellow evaders.

At the church, a man aged about thirty met the airmen, and the guides who accompanied the men on the train departed. The new guide escorted the men to a home whose occupants identified themselves only as Jacques and Madelaine. Jacques Mourlet, a wine merchant, had joined a Resistance organization that helped airmen leave France by boat. He and his wife had been married for about a year. In addition to the eight new arrivals, they were sheltering two other airmen: Armstrong's housemates from Queenie's Boarding House, Vic Matthews and Andrew Lindsay. Matthews and Lindsay relayed to the new guests that the Resistance was arranging for a fishing boat to take them to a British naval vessel in the Atlantic.

One afternoon, a man called "Fanfan" came to the Mourlets' home. Wearing a leather trench coat and hat, Fanfan—an obvious alias—looked every bit the spy. His real name was Yves Le Hénaff, a resident of Brittany whose family owned a canning plant in Quimper. Le Hénaff had served as a naval officer in Oran, Algeria, still a French colony controlled by the Vichy government, which was collaborating with the Germans. Le Hénaff despised the Nazis, so, after the British

A police raid was imminent.

and Americans invaded North Africa and took control of Oran in 1942, he agreed to go to England to learn how to help airmen escape from France. The British then parachuted him back into Brittany.

Le Hénaff explained to the men the details of the escape plan and that a British launch would be waiting for them. That afternoon, however, Mourlet learned that French police had grown suspicious of him. Too many people at his home. A police raid was imminent.

Lindsay translated Mourlet's escape plan for the other airmen. They had to be ready to flee the house. A messenger would announce if the police were coming. The men would climb through a window into the rear courtyard. Mourlet would unlock a door in the wall. Then they would walk to a nearby brook and hide in the bushes. When the police arrived, Mourlet would show them that he wasn't harboring any Allied fliers. When the police departed, he would go to the brook, blow a whistle, assemble the men, and take them to another house.

The messenger came. Mourlet and the ten airmen sprang into action. The men climbed through the window into the courtyard and were ready to go through the door in the wall—but Mourlet couldn't unlock it. In desperation, the men had to scramble *over* the seven-foot wall before hiding in the bushes.

After an hour, as planned, Mourlet went to the brook and blew a whistle. Those who heard the whistle came out. Mourlet then walked with the men to the apartment of his uncle, Abbé Corentin Lozac'hmeur, a middle-aged Catholic priest. The cleric took the men to a twelve-by-fifteen-foot room furnished with chairs, blankets, and pillows.

That's when Mourlet realized that only eight airmen were present. The other two hadn't rejoined the group. He raced downstairs to hunt for the missing men. The eight airmen and Abbé Lozac'hmeur waited, not knowing whether the police had arrested the two missing men already and were coming to the apartment to arrest everyone else.

Within an hour, Mourlet returned with the two lost men, whom he had found wandering in the town's market.

The next morning, Madelaine Mourlet and Jacques's mother, Marie, came to the apartment with bread, cheese, and fruit. Marie Mourlet hated the Nazis. When she talked about Germans, she used a pejorative term, *les Boches*—the French equivalent of "the Huns." She liked to outwit them, which she had done several times. She once hid two airmen on the first floor of her home while two German officers lodged on the second.

The airmen remained at the apartment for several days, waiting to learn when they could board the fishing boat. Early on the morning of November 5, however, Le Hénaff came to tell them that the Resistance had canceled the escape plan. The airmen had to return to Paris. The men didn't know the reason for the cancellation, but it turned out that the wife of the dock owner had persuaded her husband not to participate in the operation. Without the dock owner's approval, the boat couldn't leave.

★

DISAPPOINTED, THE TEN MEN RETURNED TO PARIS ON AN OVERNIGHT train. At the Montparnasse station, Le Hénaff quickly divided the airmen into groups of two to go with new guides. Armstrong and another American, Sergeant Robert Sheets, went with a thirty-year-old guide named Gilbert. As before, the guide spoke with French police checking identification papers as the two airmen walked by unnoticed.

Gilbert took Armstrong and Sheets to the seventh and top floor of an apartment building on Rue Saint-Merri in the center of Paris, not far from the Hôtel de Ville (city hall) and Notre Dame Cathedral. Two English airmen were also in the apartment. Gilbert Virmoux, a courier at the Sorbonne, lived here. The furniture was sparse, and the men soon grew bored—but at least they were safe. Regardless of their setback, they were more fortunate than some of their neighbors. Francis Le Calonnec and his wife lived in the unit immediately below them. If she left the building, legally she had to wear a yellow Star of David identifying her as Jewish. To lower the risk of detection, she chose to remain inside.

Later in November, Virmoux took Armstrong, Sheets, and the two British airmen to a train station where two female guides met them. The airmen and the two guides, one of whom was Denise Lenain, a student at the Sorbonne, took a train to Marles-en-Brie, a town about twenty-five miles east of Paris. From there they walked down an unpaved road.

After several hours on foot, they arrived at Château de La Fortelle at Rozay-en-Brie. The Resistance used the chateau, a majestic mansion on two hundred acres, to prepare the airmen for a grueling experience: walking over the Pyrenees, which form the natural border between France and Spain. For ten days, the men cut wood, walked the estate, and played football with a rag ball. The Resistance also fed them well. But the chateau raised more than just their fitness level: It also raised their hopes. If they could walk across the Pyrenees to Spain, another neutral country, they could return to England relatively easily.

Tears flowed from everyone's eyes.

A group of Frenchmen was staying at the chateau to take sabotage lessons. On the airmen's last full day there, the leader of the French group sat with the airmen. Armstrong asked him if he would sing the "Marseillaise," the French national anthem.

The sabotage leader, who spoke some English, declined at first. He said he couldn't sing the anthem while Nazis occupied his country. Armstrong persisted: Hearing the anthem would live in his memory long after the liberation of France.

The leader changed his mind. As he sang the chorus, *"Aux armes, citoyens!"*—To arms, citizens!—tears flowed from his eyes.

Then tears flowed from everyone's eyes.

★

THE AIRMEN RETURNED TO PARIS, WHERE THEY STAYED FOR A FEW DAYS. Andrew Lindsay and Robert Sheets swapped accommodations so that Lindsay and Armstrong lodged together at Virmoux's apartment along with two British airmen. In mid-December, Virmoux informed the four men that they would be going to the Pyrenees. The time had come.

At the Austerlitz station, the four men and their escort boarded a train for Carcassonne, a walled medieval city in the South of France. Virmoux put Armstrong and Lindsay in a compartment with an elderly couple. Lindsay could speak French in case the couple spoke to him, but Armstrong slept or pretended to sleep during much of the trip to avoid detection. At one point, Armstrong woke from actual sleep to see Lindsay smiling at him. Armstrong nodded, indicating that he wanted to talk outside the compartment. In the aisle, Armstrong asked Lindsay why he was smiling. Apparently the woman with whom they were sitting had said to her husband that she had never seen anyone sleep so much.

In Carcassonne, as the airmen left their coach, they spotted a German army officer standing at the exit gate on the station platform. Accompanied by soldiers armed with rifles, the officer was checking the passengers' identification papers. Surely the Germans would find him out, arrest him, and send him to a prison camp, Armstrong thought.

Virmoux, however, had no intention of letting that happen. He turned on his heel and directed the men to a washroom at the other end of the station. Two other airmen and their female guide were heading in the same direction. The guide was Denise Lenain, one of the women who had escorted Armstrong to the Château de La Fortelle, where the Resistance had trained the men for the journey across the Pyrenees.

The six airmen waited patiently but nervously in the washroom. Within an hour, all the other passengers and then the German soldiers departed the platform. Virmoux and Lenain led the men from the washroom and into Carcassonne.

Unfortunately their good luck didn't last. Virmoux and Lenain couldn't find the next contact, who was tasked with guiding the airmen to Spain. They shepherded the men to a restaurant in the center of town and then to a church while they sought a haven where the men could stay. The airmen subsequently went to a Red Cross building while they awaited a train to Quillan, a town in the foothills where the guide lived. But Virmoux and Lenain couldn't find the guide there, either. Without an escort, the men had no hope of crossing the forbidding mountains.

The airmen stayed in a ski lodge in Quillan overnight, and, after breakfast the next day, they began the frustrating journey back to Carcassonne and then to Paris.

★

IN CARCASSONNE, THE AIRMEN RETURNED TO THE RESTAURANT AT which they had eaten on their way to Quillan, then proceeded to the train station, which—to their immediate consternation—was crawling with German soldiers. Armstrong grew tense. But the soldiers weren't hunting for Allied airmen. They were fighting the cold by huddling near a fireplace. Not one of them bothered any of the shivering airmen.

On the train to Paris, the passengers in Armstrong's compartment tried to talk to him and Lindsay. A woman offered Armstrong an apple, but he resisted. On December 19, five days after they had departed for the Pyrenees, the men arrived back in Paris. Armstrong went directly to Virmoux's apartment, where once again he felt safe.

A day later, Virmoux informed the men that they would be leaving his apartment. He gave no reason. The Resistance didn't always explain what it was doing or why. Before the men left Rue Saint-Merri, Virmoux gave Armstrong a Christmas card depicting St. Nicholas holding a lantern, which represented hope. The note on the card said, "*A toi mon cher Jim, bon retour chez toi. Gilbert.*" To you, my dear Jim, safe travels home. Gilbert.

Soon after, Virmoux led the airmen to a nearby church and said goodbye. Several other members of the Resistance quickly came into the church. Armstrong left with a stout woman named Odette, about thirty-five years old, who told him—unnervingly—that she had no

She had no experience hiding Allied fliers.

experience hiding Allied fliers. Arm in arm, Odette took Armstrong to her apartment in Rue Valentin Haüy, which lay across the Seine halfway between the Eiffel Tower and the Montparnasse cemetery.

Odette shared her apartment with another woman, but both women worked, leaving Armstrong alone during the day. One evening, the two women walked with Armstrong to the Seine, a pleasant respite from time spent indoors. But that reprieve ended quickly. The following day, a man—possibly a senior member of the Resistance—warned Odette against taking Armstrong outside her building. The risk of being stopped and questioned vastly outweighed the benefit of a pleasant stroll.

Armstrong stayed with Odette for only a few days. On Christmas Eve, she walked with him back to the church where they had met. A young man, the next guide, collected Armstrong there, then took him to a Métro station and then a railway station. At the train station, the guide gave Armstrong a ticket to Quimper, which delighted the aviator. Quimper was the location of the failed attempt to escape by boat, but the thought of trying again raised his hopes of leaving France and going home.

On the train to Quimper, Armstrong again feigned sleep. At Le Mans, almost halfway between Paris and their destination, they transferred to another train. A curfew required residents of Le Mans to remain indoors at night, so a station attendant gave Armstrong a note permitting him to wait for the next train. Sitting on a bench in the waiting area, Armstrong noticed several familiar faces: airmen who had been with him on his trip to the Pyrenees.

Armstrong fell asleep. In the middle of the night, a policeman kicked his feet and startled him awake. Armstrong showed the officer his identity card, but the policeman shook his head. In his sleepy haze, the airman remembered that the station attendant had given him a permission slip to remain at the station. The officer examined it, handed it back, and moved on to the other passengers. Armstrong felt relieved. "Jean Riber" was safe. For now.

★

WHEN THE TRAIN ARRIVED AT QUIMPER, STATION WORKERS ATTACHED Armstrong's coach to a train going to Tréboul, a seaside town about ten miles away.

In the morning, two women in the Resistance met the six airmen at the Tréboul station and led them past a bay where fishermen worked on their nets and into a pine-laden residential area. In a house there, young Frenchmen warmly welcomed the group. It was Christmas Day.

Noel Le Guillou, leader of the house group, told the aviators that they formed part of a larger group leaving that evening on a boat bound for England. Le Guillou had divided the larger group of thirty men into two subgroups. The first walked to the bay immediately. The second group, which included the airmen, departed half an hour later.

As Armstrong's group walked to the bay, they spotted four German troops cycling toward them. Armstrong and his comrades quickly ducked behind a sign. The Germans didn't see them—but it was a close call.

At the shore, Armstrong took off his shoes and socks, rolled up his pants, and waded to *La Jeanne*, their escape vessel. Just as he was about

An airman already on the boat spoke the only words that Armstrong didn't want to hear.

to climb on board, an airman already on the boat spoke the only words that Armstrong didn't want to hear: "Turn around, go back. The escape is off!"

The boat couldn't depart; it needed fuel. Someone had locked the fuel storage area, and the crew didn't have a key. The men returned to the house in the pines and stayed overnight.

When Armstrong awoke, all the Frenchmen had gone back to their own homes. Some of the other airmen were making breakfast.

Outside, a woman screamed, shattering the morning calm. One of the aviators who understood French quickly translated: Police! Police! Robbers!

If the police came sniffing for thieves, no one wanted to have to answer their questions. The men raced out through the back door to a wooded area, where they hid quietly in a drainage ditch. After an hour, Le Guillou collected them. Apparently a neighbor had seen people in the house and thought *they* were robbers. Le Guillou explained to the woman that the owner of the property had given him permission to use the house.

But the house was no longer safe. Neighbors sympathetic to the Nazis might make inquiries about who was tromping around in it.

In the morning, Le Guillou found new accommodations for the airmen in Tréboul and the nearby town of Douarnenez. He took Armstrong and Warrant Officer Russell Jones to a room above a dry

Outside, a woman screamed, shattering the morning calm.

goods store in the latter town. Armstrong and the tall, blond Canadian remained in the room with the drapes pulled in case someone on the street below caught sight of them.

★

ON NEW YEAR'S EVE, THE TWO MEN AWOKE TO THE SOUNDS OF TOWNS-folk celebrating as best they could while Nazi troops occupied their country. As they marched along a street, the residents heartily sang the French version of a well-known British song: *"La Route Est Longue jusqu'à Tipperary,"* "It's a Long Way to Tipperary." As he listened to the jubilation, Armstrong hoped that the new year would see him home soon. He had spent a great deal of time thinking about how to get back to Bradenton.

On New Year's Day, Le Guillou took Armstrong and Jones to a safer location. Across the street, they walked up to the third-floor apartment of Evelyn Malhomme, who—despite the risk she was taking—didn't mind that Armstrong and Jones knew her full name. She wanted to help the Resistance however she could.

Madame Malhomme was living on her own now. Her husband, Maurice, was in a German concentration camp, and her two sons were serving with the Free French forces. She treated Armstrong and Jones as though they were her sons. She cooked fine meals for them and taught them French words, such as *choux-fleur* when they were eating cauliflower.

At Madame Malhomme's apartment, the two men passed the time by playing cards at the kitchen table. Every so often, Armstrong turned to gaze through a window at the beauty of Douarnenez Bay. It reminded him of Tampa Bay, just a few blocks from his home.

★

AS THE NEW YEAR RECEDED, ARMSTRONG WONDERED WHETHER THE Resistance would ever find a boat to take him to England. On most days, he and Jones heard German guns firing from a point near the bay. They couldn't tell whether Nazi troops were conducting target practice or firing at Allied ships.

On January 20, Madame Malhomme told the two men that the Resistance had arranged for a fishing boat to take them to England the following day. She gave Armstrong a few mementoes to take with him. One was a five-franc note on which she had written a few words of encouragement: *"Bonne chance—20-1-44."* Good luck, January 20, 1944.

★

THE RESISTANCE HAD ARRANGED FOR GABRIEL CLOAREC, CAPTAIN OF A fishing boat, to ferry Allied airmen and Frenchmen to England aboard the *Breiz-Izel*, the Breton term for Lower Brittany. Cloarec had the *Breiz-Izel* towed up an estuary away from the bay, telling his fellow fishermen that he was moving the boat for repairs. In actuality, he was moving it closer to a dock from which the passengers could board the vessel.

Several residents of Douarnenez brought fuel to the boat in wheelbarrows and baby carriages. That evening, thirty-one men, including Cloarec and his crew, quietly boarded the *Breiz-Izel*. The passengers filed through the hatch and into the hold. They had to lie down because there wasn't enough room between the floor and the deck to stand or sit.

In the early hours of January 22, the crew untied the ropes holding the ship to the dock. The men in the hold felt the boat move. Armstrong hoped that this time he finally would make it back to England. The *Breiz-Izel* gently drifted to sea with the tide as the crew used an oar to steer the boat. Cloarec didn't start the engine because he didn't want the noise to alert the French guards patrolling the harbor or the German troops operating the heavy guns near the bay.

The men on the boat kept quiet. If they spoke, they whispered. One man popped his head through the hatch to see what was happening, but the ink-black night and low, thick clouds shrouded all.

Then came a shout from onshore. Armstrong thought it was an order to halt, but a French guard who spoke Breton had yelled, *"Al laer! Al laer!"* Thief! Thief! The guard thought someone was stealing the fishing boat. German troops at the mouth of the bay heard the guard's alarm and switched on a searchlight, but they saw nothing.

Cloarec stoically let the boat drift farther out to sea before starting the engine. Within a few hours, the sea became rough, and strong winds blew from the southwest. The *Breiz-Izel* was pushing into a gale. Water sloshed into the hold, and the men grew seasick. The winds blew so fiercely that night that the British Royal Navy held its ships in port—but

Turning back meant certain death for all aboard.

Cloarec had no choice but to continue sailing. Turning back meant certain death for all aboard.

Eventually the storm abated. The men in the hold clambered onto the deck, and their eyes fell on England's blessed shore. Relief washed over everyone. The British passengers were home; the French were safe; and those from the other side of the Atlantic were on their way home. As a British patrol launch approached, the crew hoisted British and French flags up the mast.

"Who are you?" a sailor on the launch asked, puzzled.

One of the men told the sailor who they were.

"Follow us," the sailor said.

The *Breiz-Izel* followed the launch to Falmouth Harbor.

Finally—after four and a half months in France and thirty-six hours traversing the English Channel—Second Lieutenant James Armstrong found himself once again on English soil, grateful that the captain and crew of the *Breiz-Izel* had showed both the courage and skill to make such a perilous voyage.

★

THE STUTTGART RAID THAT LED TO ARMSTRONG'S LONG ORDEAL IN France failed to achieve its purpose. Heavy cloud cover prevented the crew of the lead bomber from locating the VKF ball-bearing plant,

When she received the message, she burst into tears and wept with joy.

and German fighters successfully attacked many of the 338 B-17s that participated in the raid. The AAF lost forty-five bombers in the raid.

On January 29, 1944—more than four months after he had been classified as missing in action—Armstrong telegrammed his mother to let her know he was well and coming home. When she received the message, she burst into tears and wept with joy.

On February 1, Armstrong landed in Washington, DC, in the middle of a snowstorm, delighted to be back in the United States. He took a train to Florida, and, when he arrived in Bradenton, it felt to him as though the entire city was welcoming him home.

★

AFTER THE WAR, ARMSTRONG RETURNED TO COLLEGE. INSTEAD OF picking up where he had stopped at Georgia Tech, he studied agriculture at the University of Florida, then worked for a fertilizer company after graduation.

But as the years passed, he felt a calling, and in 1960 he became a minister with the Presbyterian Church, eventually setting up his own place of worship, the New Covenant Church in Thomasville, Georgia.

In the years after the war, Armstrong tried to forget what had happened. But with the passing of time, his curiosity—about what had happened to his crew, his comrades in France, and the members of the French Resistance who had protected him—grew. He contacted members of his crew and visited France several times to search for clues.

Every member of Armstrong's crew survived the war, except of course for James Redwing, who was killed during the Stuttgart flight. Six members of the crew became prisoners of war, and three, including Armstrong, successfully evaded the Germans. Redwing is buried at the Epinal American Cemetery in Dinozé, France.

Olen Grant, who survived when *Yankee Raider* landed, unpiloted, in the sugar beet field, became a prisoner of war. For medical reasons, the Germans permitted him to return to America in February 1945.

On his return visits to France, Armstrong learned the full details of many of the incidents in which he was involved, such as the voyage of the *Breiz-Izel* from Douarnenez to Falmouth. He also learned the names of many members of the Resistance, who for safety reasons hadn't identified themselves fully during the war.

Yves Le Hénaff, the naval officer who arranged unsuccessfully for a boat to go to England on Christmas Day 1943, was arrested by the Germans. He died en route to a concentration camp. Annie Price, who had helped Armstrong in Triel-sur-Seine, wrote to Armstrong after the Allies liberated France, describing the hardships of postwar France. Alec Prochiantz, a medical intern at the time, later became a doctor. After the war, Dr. Prochiantz studied medicine in America before returning to France. Gabriel Cloarec, captain of the *Breiz-Izel*, joined the Free French forces after arriving in England.

On a trip to France in 1994, Armstrong met the ambulance driver who took Olen Grant to a hospital after he emerged from *Yankee Raider*. On another trip ten years later, Armstrong retrieved his parachute,

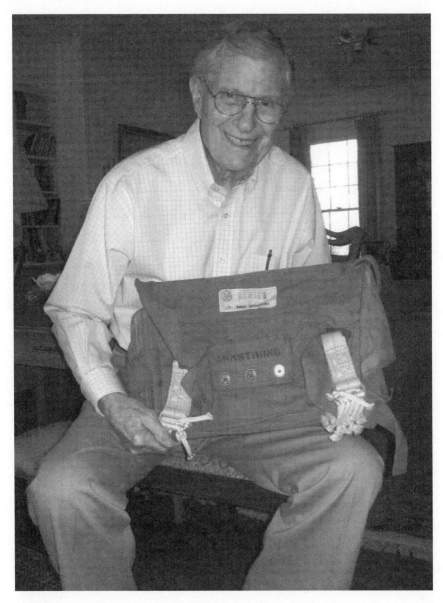

James Armstrong holds his parachute in 2010.

which Robert Stoner, his copilot, had given to Alfred Mourette. The Mourette family had kept the chute for several generations. A few pieces of it were missing, however. They had become lingerie.

Armstrong never did locate some of his guides, such as Gilbert Virmoux or Noel Le Guillou. Nor was he able to contact Théodorine Quénot, the woman whom he and his roommates had affectionately called Queenie. Armstrong made contact with some of the Allied airmen who had been with him in France, such as Vic Matthews and Russell Jones. In 2008, Armstrong reunited with Denise Lenain—who had served as his guide twice—at the Mighty Eighth Air Force Museum in Savannah, Georgia.

Armstrong and his wife, Nita, later moved to Lawrenceville, Georgia, taking with them his souvenirs of the time he spent with the Resistance, such as the Christmas card from Gilbert Virmoux and the five-franc note from Evelyn Malhomme. They still serve as tangible reminders of the men and women who risked their lives to help a young American aviator who took the long way home.

"I shall never forget," Armstrong said. "Freedom is not free."

6

LOCKED IN PLACE

BETTY GUILD
6th Ferrying Group
Air Transport Command
US Army Air Forces

AMELIA EARHART SPOKE AT THE UNIVERSITY OF HAWAII IN Honolulu on January 3, 1935. Sitting in the front row was fourteen-year-old Betty Guild, who had a keen and growing interest in aviation. The famous flier delivered her speech and walked over to Betty, who delighted in meeting her. Earhart invited Betty to watch her take off from Wheeler Field for a flight to Oakland, California. After some persuasion, Betty's father, Archibald, drove her to the airport a week and a half later to watch the momentous event.

That brief encounter with Earhart inspired Betty to learn to fly. When not on duty, a Navy pilot based at Pearl Harbor offered her lessons, taking her up in a dual-control plane. Betty also took flying lessons at a private airfield. To pay for them, she did bookkeeping for the airfield. At the time, her parents knew nothing about either set of lessons. She told them she was going to the beach—and went to the airfield instead.

Betty earned her private pilot's license and became a commercial pilot and flying instructor. She also flew tourists on sightseeing trips around the Hawaiian Islands. She had arranged one such flight for Sunday, December 7, 1941. The tourist canceled the early morning flight, however, and rebooked for the following day.

On Saturday, December 6, Betty attended a party at an officers' club at Pearl Harbor with Robert Tackaberry, an ensign aboard the USS *California*, a battleship. She had never had alcohol before, but

That brief encounter with Earhart inspired Betty to learn to fly.

that night she imbibed some Southern Comfort. Later that evening, Tackaberry drove her home to Keeaumoku Street in Honolulu, some twenty miles away. Archibald Guild persuaded the ensign to stay overnight rather than drive all the way back to the *California*.

The next morning, Japanese planes attacked the base in the harbor as well as nearby airfields. Betty's brothers, Thornton and Robert, could see the planes from their home.

But the Southern Comfort had given Betty a hangover. When she heard the roaring of aircraft engines overhead, she wanted to go back to sleep, but her brothers woke her up. From a second-floor balcony, they witnessed the planes with red suns painted on their wings. Smoke was rising from Pearl Harbor and Kaimuki, a neighborhood where Chinese and Japanese immigrants lived. Betty Guild knew that the Japanese aircraft were flying exactly where she would have been flying if the tourist hadn't canceled the morning's flight.

Tackaberry understandably wanted to return to Pearl Harbor as quickly as possible. Archibald Guild offered to drive him to the harbor even though Japanese pilots were firing at vehicles on Hawaii's roads. The two men arrived at their destination without being strafed, but Tackaberry soon learned that the Japanese had torpedoed the *California*. His roommate had died.

In one startling moment, Hawaii had become a war zone. The days when Betty could fly tourists around the idyllic islands had come to an

---

In one startling moment, Hawaii had become a war zone.

---

abrupt end. Radio stations warned Hawaiians that the Japanese might attack again. Residents feared the worst and implemented blackouts.

A cousin in the Navy suggested that Betty find work as a naval secretary at Pearl Harbor. She applied, quickly landed the job, and spent her time logging the locations of American and Japanese ships in the Pacific. A few months later, she married Robert Tackaberry and went with him to Philadelphia, where he took training courses before returning to the Pacific.

★

IN PEACETIME, THE US ARMY AIR FORCES DIDN'T TRAIN WOMEN TO FLY military planes. But of course the events of December 7, 1941, changed everything. In order to fight an air war against Japan and another against Germany, America needed more pilots—regardless of gender. The Army Air Forces (AAF) decided to use qualified women pilots for noncombat tasks, such as moving planes around the country.

The AAF established two independent branches for women: the Women's Auxiliary Ferrying Squadron and the Women's Flying Training Detachment. The ferrying squadron contacted Betty but ultimately didn't recruit her because she had no experience flying multi-engine aircraft. The training detachment subsequently invited her to attend its first course, which took place in Houston in 1942. Despite their sensitive and essential paramilitary duties, women pilots didn't qualify as members of the armed forces. Neither did they receive the benefits granted to male pilots. They ranked merely as civil servants. (If killed on duty, the women weren't entitled to a military funeral.) But Betty Tackaberry was thrilled to be flying again—even though she felt

---

The women pilots didn't qualify as members of the armed forces. They ranked merely as civil servants.

---

the male instructors were treating the women students like guinea pigs in some bizarre experiment.

She graduated in spring 1943 and relocated soon afterward to Long Beach Army Air Base in Southern California, where she flew with the 6th Ferrying Group of the Air Transport Command. The base became home to as many as forty women pilots, and Barbara Erickson served as their commander.

★

IN 1943, BETTY CLIMBED INTO A P-39 AIRACOBRA AT NIAGARA FALLS, NEW York, for a long trip to Great Falls, Montana. She stopped at Chicago before continuing again the next morning.

The sky was clear, and the flight from Chicago seemed routine. At 16,000 feet over Minnesota, the instrument panel showed that all systems were working properly. But Betty lurched in shock and then fear when, over her right shoulder, she saw black smoke spewing from the back of the plane.

Fire might cause an explosion. She needed to land as quickly as possible. She knew the Mayo Clinic at Rochester, Minnesota, used a nearby airfield, so she flew straight to it and brought the P-39 down.

Mechanics at the airfield examined the plane. The engine had

They couldn't believe that she had been able to land with an engine in such condition.

---

burned so badly that it had turned black. They couldn't believe that she had been able to land with an engine in such condition. Not wanting to tempt fate a second time so soon after, Betty returned to Long Beach on a commercial flight.

★

IN LATE 1943, WHILE DELIVERING A P-51 MUSTANG FROM LONG BEACH TO Newark, New Jersey, Betty planned to stop at an airport near Dallas. As she approached, she pushed the lever on the instrument panel to lower the wheels. A green light should have lit up to show that the wheels had descended and had locked in place—but the light didn't go on. Betty radioed the control tower and asked the controllers to look at the wheels as she flew by. The left wheel had come down properly, but the right wheel remained in the fuselage. The controllers advised her to spin the plane in order to make the right wheel drop.

Betty turned the plane over and heard the right wheel drop. But the green light for that wheel still didn't light up, which meant that it might not have locked into the proper position. The controllers advised her to bail out, indicating where to fly the plane so that it didn't cause problems when it crashed. Betty decided to land at the airport, however, despite the dubious wheel.

To avoid a situation in which the unlocked wheel collapsed on touchdown, Betty needed to make as straight a landing as possible. Doing so ensured that landing exerted no pressure on either side of the right wheel.

She touched down and rolled the P-51 along the runway. An emergency truck followed her, but in the end she didn't need any emergency assistance. She made what she later called "probably the straightest landing in my life." The right wheel remained in position.

After the plane stopped, the ground crew inserted a pole between the two wheels to stop them from collapsing as Betty taxied the plane to a hangar for further inspection. They determined that, in fact, the right wheel hadn't locked into place.

★

DURING THE WAR, THE AAF NEVER PUBLICLY DISCUSSED WHAT THE women pilots were doing. As a result, many Americans didn't even know that women pilots were flying military aircraft. Betty learned this the hard way in Redding, California. She had landed in the sleepy Northern California city to wait for the weather to clear so she could continue a flight to McChord Field in Tacoma, Washington. She and two other women pilots—all wearing flight suits—were doing some leisurely window shopping that Sunday. The wife of a male pilot at the Redding air base spotted the women and called the police because she thought they were impersonating pilots.

Back at their hotel, the women opened the door to their room and found the sheriff sitting on one of the beds.

"Hello, girls," he said. "Come on in."

"Hello, girls," he said. "Come on in."

The three pilots showed their identification cards to the sheriff, but he openly doubted their authenticity. He drove them to the police station. There the women insisted that the sheriff call their base in Long Beach, which he did.

"Never heard of them," the person who answered the phone told the sheriff, who was growing more skeptical of the women's story.

Betty insisted that he call the base again to speak to an officer on duty. The sheriff obliged her, spoke to an officer, and learned that the women really were who they said they were. He apologized to Betty and the other two pilots, offering to buy them dinner. The women declined, choosing instead to hit a bar to have a few drinks.

Nor was the sheriff alone in doubting that women were flying as part of the war effort. Even some male pilots didn't know that American women were flying military aircraft. On another flight from Long Beach to Newark, Betty heard male pilots on her radio, telling crude jokes.

When she made a comment, one of the men expressed his surprise: "Hey, sounded like a gal's voice on the radio."

"No! How can a gal be on a military frequency?" one of the other men asked.

Betty explained how and why she had access to a military frequency.

The male pilots apologized to Betty for their crass humor and invited her to land at their base in Las Vegas so they could take her out for dinner. She declined that invitation as well because she needed to continue flying to Newark, where the plane she was flying would be loaded onto a ship and sent to Europe.

★

IN AUGUST 1943, THE AAF CONSOLIDATED THE FERRYING SQUADRON AND the training detachment into a new organization: the Women Airforce Service Pilots, which became known by the acronym WASP. But roughly a year later, Congress saw little need for it to continue because the AAF needed fewer new pilots. WASP closed down.

General Hap Arnold, commander of the Army Air Forces, told the last WASP class that they had shown they could fly "wingtip to wingtip with your brothers." He added, "If ever there was a doubt in anyone's mind that women could become skilled pilots, the WASPs dispelled that doubt."

Before that farewell speech, though, General Arnold had demonstrated his respect for women fliers by awarding the Air Medal to Barbara Erickson, the women's commander at the Long Beach Army Air Base. She had earned the medal—given for achievements accomplished in flight—by completing five transcontinental flights in just four days.

The 1,074 women who graduated from the WASP program flew

"If ever there was a doubt in anyone's mind that women could become skilled pilots, the WASPs dispelled that doubt."

millions of miles while delivering 13,000 aircraft during the war. Erickson understood that flying during the war in noncombat roles was dangerous. Ferrying planes had its own risks: 90 percent of the aircraft that her squadron flew hadn't been flown before. Some thirty-eight women pilots died either in training or on duty. Six of them belonged to Erickson's squadron.

The end of the WASPs dealt a devastating and heartbreaking blow to Erickson, who noted sadly that hundreds of planes needing to be flown to the East Coast sat idle on the tarmac.

The decision also disappointed Betty Tackaberry. She stayed at Long Beach and served as an instructor of a Link Trainer, a simulated aircraft used to train pilots. After divorcing Robert, Betty married George Blake, who had served as a pilot with the AAF, and moved to Arizona.

Since then, the accomplishments of the WASP fliers have met with considerably more public recognition and praise. In 1977, Congress granted the women pilots the status of veterans, and in 2009 it collectively awarded them the Congressional Gold Medal. The following year, Betty Blake attended the presentation ceremony in Washington, DC.

"I just didn't believe it," she said from her home in Scottsdale, Arizona.

Simultaneous legislation enabled the WASPs to receive veterans' benefits, but it didn't grant them status with the armed services. As a result, they still don't have the right to be buried at Arlington National Cemetery. Spurred by the request of WASP Elaine Harmon to have her ashes placed there, retired Air Force colonel and US representative Martha McSally of Arizona introduced legislation in 2016 to extend that right to the women pilots.

★

Betty Blake holds a model of her favorite plane, the P-51 Mustang, in 2012.

AFTER THE WASP CEASED TO EXIST, FORMER SQUADRON COMMANDER Barbara Erickson married Jack London, also a pilot, and maintained her interest in aviation. In 1976, their daughter Terry became Western Airlines' first woman pilot. One of Terry's daughters, Kelly, also became a pilot and flew her mother and grandmother from San Jose, California, to Washington, DC, for the medal presentation ceremony. Barbara London died in 2013.

"I didn't feel that anything I did was a sacrifice," said Betty Blake of her time as a WASP. "It was an opportunity." She bravely seized that opportunity and urged young women to do the same and aim high. "There's just no limit to what women can do today."

Betty Blake died in 2015.

THE SALUTE

CHARLES BROWN
Second Lieutenant
527th Bombardment
Squadron
379th Bomb Group
US Army Air Forces

S ECOND LIEUTENANT CHARLES BROWN WOKE UP EARLY ON December 20, 1943. The twenty-two-year-old pilot from Weston, West Virginia, belonged to the Army Air Forces' 379th Bomb Group, based at Kimbolton, near Cambridge, England. Their target that morning was an aircraft factory near Bremen in northwest Germany.

Brown flew his B-17, called *Ye Olde Pub*, at 27,300 feet. About ten minutes away from the target, German anti-aircraft flak damaged two of the plane's four engines and blew a large hole in its Plexiglas nose. Brutally cold air—minus-76 degrees—poured into the plane.

Shortly after the crew dropped their bomb load, fifteen German fighters spotted the struggling aircraft and attacked from the front and the rear. Desperate to escape, Brown turned the plane sharply from side to side, but it rolled upside down and plunged toward the ground. Seeing the bomber about to crash, the German pilots halted their attack.

Brown had lost consciousness but came to just in time—less than five hundred feet from the ground. In a flash, he leveled the aircraft, but the damaged bomber could fly only slightly faster than stalling speed, about 100 miles an hour. Still, that was fast enough to keep *Ye Olde Pub* in the air so they could wing it out of Germany.

Over the flat pasture land near Wilhelmshaven, the controls became problematic. The rudder pedals on the floor weren't responding. Brown sent his copilot, Second Lieutenant Spencer "Pinky" Luke, and the upper-turret gunner, Staff Sergeant Bertrand "Frenchy" Coulombe, to check on the problem. The news was dire. Cannon shells had struck the radio room, knocking out the intercom and radio equipment. Another shell somehow had pierced the right wing without exploding and had

The blood and sweat on his face froze, sealing his oxygen mask to his skin.

just missed a fuel tank. A third engine wasn't functioning properly, and only one of the aircraft's eleven guns worked. *Ye Olde Pub* was hobbling hard and virtually defenseless.

The German attack had killed the tail gunner, Staff Sergeant Hugh "Ecky" Eckenrode, and shattered the left leg of Sergeant Alex Yelesanko, the left gunner. Bullet fragments had lodged in the eye of the radio operator, Staff Sergeant Richard Pechout, and also in Brown's right shoulder. The right gunner, Sergeant Lloyd Jennings, had a severely bruised leg, and Second Lieutenant Al Sadok, the navigator, had a cut forehead. Brown's injury wasn't serious, but in the intense cold the blood and sweat on his face froze, sealing his oxygen mask to his skin. Several crewmembers, including Pechout and Sergeant Sam Blackford, the lower-turret gunner, were developing severe frostbite.

They were still about 250 miles from England and had to cross the North Sea. If Brown couldn't keep the plane in the air, ditching in the cold, rough water was hardly a better option. What he didn't know was that they were moving into exceptionally dangerous airspace. *Ye Olde Pub* was about to fly over Jever Air Base, a Luftwaffe bomber base.

★

FIRST LIEUTENANT FRANZ STIGLER, A GERMAN PILOT FROM FIGHTER WING Jagdgeschwader 27, based in Wiesbaden, was standing on the Jever field

Franz Stigler during the war.

beside his Messerschmitt 109, which the ground crew was refueling and rearming. It was around noon, and Stigler wanted to fly again. He had shot down two B-17s that morning. If he shot down one more that day, he'd receive the Knight's Cross, one of Germany's highest honors.

As he waited, Stigler saw a B-17 fly over a wooded area and then over the edge of the airfield. The bomber was flying so low that he wondered whether it had just taken off. *Noch einer für mich*, he thought. Another one for me. Before the ground crew had time to finish, he climbed back into the cockpit and raced into the sky.

Stigler had studied to be a monk and made his first solo flight at age twelve at the monastery glider club. He later pursued aeronautical engineering and became a pilot with Lufthansa, Germany's national airline. When the war started, Stigler joined the Luftwaffe and served as a pilot instructor. After his brother August, a fighter pilot, was killed in 1940, he volunteered for active duty.

As the B-17 limped along, Stigler approached it from the rear, ready to fire if anyone so much as pointed a gun in his direction. Within six

He climbed back into the cockpit and raced into the sky.

Blood was running down the barrels of the rear guns.

yards of the bomber, he could see the damage to the tail. The rear gunner wasn't moving, and blood was running down the barrels of the rear guns. Moving along the bomber's right side, he could see the crew helping one of their comrades through the holes in the fuselage. They were trying to administer morphine to Yelesanko, the left gunner, but in the freezing cold the morphine had turned into a gel that didn't flow freely.

Stigler flew forward, positioning himself alongside the B-17's cockpit. Brown spotted the aircraft bearing a swastika flying with him. He closed his eyes for a moment. When he opened them, the plane was still there. It was flying so close that the tip of its left wing hovered only a few feet away from the tip of their own wing. Brown could see the German pilot's eyes.

Stigler nodded. Brown didn't know what to do. Nothing in his training had prepared him for this.

Was the fighter out of ammunition? No, even an unarmed German pilot wouldn't fly this close to an Allied plane. Was the fighter going to deploy some secret weapon to destroy them? He'd had more than enough time, but so far nothing.

In the freezing cold the morphine had turned into a gel.

"Get up there and scare that bandit away!"

Brown couldn't determine the German pilot's motives, but he understood the hand signal pointing down. The pilot wanted him to land—but he wasn't going to surrender. The fighter pilot persisted, pulling ahead of the bomber a few times. Brown refused. Then the German pilot pointed northeast, but Brown didn't understand what he meant. By now, *Ye Olde Pub* was flying over the North Sea.

Copilot Pinky and upper-turret gunner Frenchy returned to the cockpit and saw the German fighter. They, too, were stunned.

"Get up there and scare that bandit away!" Brown said to Frenchy, urging the gunner to return to his turret and point his gun at the fighter.

He looked again at the German plane, and, much to his amazement, the pilot gave him a friendly salute, dived to the right, and disappeared.

★

BROWN CLIMBED TO ABOUT 1,000 FEET, HUGGING THE ISLANDS OFF THE German coast in case he had to make a crash landing. None of the crew wanted him to fly back over the mainland so they could bail. Anyone not injured looked after the wounded and helped Brown fly the plane. They had trained together, and they were going to stay together.

Brown flew parallel to the islands as far as he could, then headed northeast for England. *Ye Olde Pub* gradually lost altitude. Below 1,000 feet, Brown saw the rough, dull gray whitecaps of the North Sea. Ditching would

They had trained together, and they were going to stay together.

be difficult. He ordered the crew to jettison anything movable to lighten the load. They tossed out guns, ammunition, oxygen equipment, and parts of the wrecked radio system. The altimeter dropped to 500 feet, then 400.

Other Allied bombers flew high above him on their way back from Germany. Brown envied them. Several P-47 Thunderbolts flew close and waggled their wings to signal that they recognized his plight. Brown hoped that they had alerted Air-Sea Rescue units. At this point, he was relying on more than just his training and his experience. He was desperately praying to see land.

The needle dropped to 300 feet.

Suddenly, at about 250 feet, something appeared on the horizon. It was a rocky shore. It was England.

Two P-47s flanked the bomber as it flew over the coast. They climbed to about 1,000 feet and circled to indicate an airfield below. He rocked his wings—lightly—to thank the P-47s for their help.

"Gear down," Brown told Frenchy.

As they approached the runway, Brown and Pinky cut the engines. *Ye Olde Pub* glided to a safe landing.

Something appeared on the horizon. It was England.

★

BACK IN GERMANY, STIGLER RETURNED TO JEVER AIR BASE BUT SAID nothing to anyone about the American bomber. If senior Luftwaffe officers learned that he hadn't shot down an American bomber, they would court-martial and execute him.

★

YE OLDE PUB HAD LANDED AT SEETHING AIRFIELD NEAR GREAT YARMOUTH, home of the 448th Bomb Group, which flew B-24s. Brown dropped down through the front hatch and slumped to the tarmac. The ground crew helped three injured airmen—Yelesanko, Pechout, and Blackford—from the plane into ambulances. They also removed Hugh Eckenrode's body.

"You're wounded," a medic said, urging Brown onto a stretcher.

"No, I'm not," he replied.

He and the rest of the crew were taken to a debriefing session. Colonel James M. Thompson, commander of the 448th, took Brown back to the aircraft. Brown couldn't believe his own eyes. When he looked at the tail—or what was left of it—he understood why he hadn't been able to control the plane.

"Lieutenant, why would you try to fly an aircraft damaged this badly?" Thompson asked.

"Sir, I had one already dead and three who could not survive a bailout," Brown replied. "Besides, I didn't know that the tail had been shot off the aircraft."

"I didn't know that the tail had been shot off the aircraft."

"Young man, I'm going to recommend you for our nation's highest award."

Brown asked about his crew. Thompson assured him that they would be taken care of, which Brown took to mean that they also would receive official recognition for their heroism.

Within hours, base officials classified the aircraft as top secret. They confiscated the film of all photos taken of the plane. A telegram from Seething to the crew's home base said nothing about an encounter with a German pilot. Back at Kimbolton, no one spoke to them about their ordeal.

★

A FEW WEEKS LATER, BROWN FLEW ON A DIFFERENT BOMBER WITH A mostly new crew. Yelesanko's left leg was amputated, but Blackford returned to active duty after two weeks. Brown completed his last combat flight on April 11, 1944. Operating from Northern Ireland, he

Base officials classified the aircraft as top secret.

ferried American planes around Great Britain. In mid-August of that year he boarded a ship back to America.

★

FRANZ STIGLER JOINED THE JAGDVERBAND 44 SQUADRON, AN ELITE GROUP of pilots who flew the Messerschmitt Me 262, a new jet fighter. Officials never learned what he had done or not done with the American bomber. He was never court-martialed. He was stationed at a German base near Salzburg, Austria, when the war ended in May 1945.

After returning to civilian life, he worked for a branch of the Messerschmitt company that made knitting looms. But postwar Germany was a dreary place, particularly for an energetic man like him. In 1953, he emigrated to Canada, where he had a relative, hoping to work on the Canadian Avro Arrow fighter plane. But the Arrow was a military plane, which meant he had to reside in Canada for two years before he could touch it. He didn't want to wait. Instead, he made his way to the Queen Charlotte Islands in British Columbia, where he worked for a logging company in their truck and boat repair shop. In 1971, he settled down in a large, tree-shaded home in a Vancouver suburb.

★

BROWN ATTENDED WEST VIRGINIA WESLEYAN COLLEGE, GRADUATED IN 1949, and rejoined the US Air Force. He primarily served in intelligence and counterintelligence and took early retirement from the military in 1965 before joining the State Department as a diplomat. After retiring in Washington, DC, in 1972, he moved to Miami and set up an energy and environmental research company.

In 1986, at a reunion of Air Force veterans in Las Vegas, Brown was chatting with former fliers about unusual incidents they had experienced or seen. When his turn came, Brown told of the German pilot who had saluted him. The group laughed and wanted to know more.

Brown set out to discover the pilot's identity, whether he survived the war, and why he hadn't shot them down. He searched records of the 448th Bomb Group, British newspapers, and museums in England and America. He found nothing. He contacted German historians, but no records of the encounter existed because Stigler had never spoken of it.

In the fall of 1989, Brown sent a letter to *Jagerblatt*, a newsletter sent to Luftwaffe pilots, asking if anyone knew about that flight on December 20, 1943. A few months later, Brown received a letter bearing a Canadian stamp. It was a letter from Franz Stigler. "I was the one," he wrote.

Brown tracked down Stigler's phone number and called him. "Convince me," he said.

Stigler described the location, the plane's condition, and the aircraft's markings, such as the *K* on the tail, the letter of the 379th Bomb Group.

"It has to be you," Brown admitted.

"It has to be you," Brown admitted.

They met in Seattle in 1990 and answered each other's questions. Stigler had never seen a plane so badly damaged but still flying. Firing on an aircraft in that condition would have been like shooting at a man in a parachute. When Stigler had pointed northeast, he was directing Brown to fly to Sweden, a neutral country. He didn't think the bomber could make it all the way back to England.

Brown and Stigler became close friends, visiting each other and talking on the phone every week. With Brown's assistance, Stigler became an honorary member of the 379th Bomb Group. He received several humanitarian awards and honors from veterans' organizations. Brown thought the Air Force had censored his flight because it didn't want to publicize a German pilot sparing the lives of an American crew, but in 2008 the Air Force finally acknowledged what Brown and his crew had achieved that cold December night and awarded him the Air Force Cross. Brown received the Cross in recognition of his extraordinary heroism, and his crew received the Silver Star for their gallantry. Staff Sergeant Hugh Eckenrode, the rear gunner, posthumously received the Distinguished Flying Cross.

Stigler's decision not to take down *Ye Olde Pub* ultimately showed the world something more important than the Knight's Cross that he would have received. He provided a shining example of honor in combat and proof that today's combatants can become tomorrow's friends.

He provided a shining example of honor in combat and proof that today's combatants can become tomorrow's friends.

Charles Brown in 2007.

Franz Stigler in 2007.

Charles Brown and Franz Stigler both died in 2008.

NATURAL FLYER

ROBERT QUERNS
Flight Officer
39th Fighter Squadron
35th Fighter Group
Fifth Air Force
US Army Air Forces

"THEY CAN'T DO THAT TO US!" SAID ROBERT QUERNS AS HE listened to the radio at his family's home in Lockport, New York. The young man who had flown model airplanes from the third-floor window of his house on Walnut Street as a boy immediately went to the town's post office to pick up enlistment papers. But the post office's doors were shut. In his eagerness, Querns had forgotten that it was closed on Sundays. He had to wait a day before he could serve his country.

When Querns returned home from the post office, his mother urged him to exercise patience. The twenty-year-old, who had been working part-time jobs after graduating from high school, accepted her advice and took a little time before filing the papers that led him to Jones Field in Bonham, Texas.

★

IN 1943, JUST BEFORE GRADUATION FROM THE PRIMARY AVIATION SCHOOL at Jones Field, Querns learned that he needed twenty more minutes in the air to reach the required sixty-five hours. An instructor volunteered to fly with him.

They took off in a Fairchild PT-19, an open-cockpit plane. Querns sat in the front. Behind him sat the instructor, who wanted to demonstrate the "falling leaf" maneuver.

"This is the way you can lose altitude if you have to," the instructor said through the Gosport tube, a communication device.

From about 2,000 feet, the plane swiftly descended toward the brown terrain. The instructor pulled up at just 100 feet above the ground. But

The PT-19 was vibrating so much that Querns couldn't read the instrument panel.

he didn't see the electrical wires running 200 feet above the ground. The plane struck the quarter-inch wire, which wrapped around the center of the propeller. The aircraft stalled momentarily—but continued flying.

The wire had slashed the left wing, creating a foot-square hole, and it knocked out the Pitot tube, an instrument that determines airspeed. The plane vibrated, and the plywood wing hummed.

"You got it," the instructor said to Querns, meaning that he wanted Querns, who could see better from the front seat, to fly the aircraft. The PT-19 was vibrating so much that Querns couldn't read the instrument panel, but he wasn't fearful. He just kept flying. He knew they were only minutes away from the airport.

"Give me another five minutes," he said, as if to the plane.

Querns flew straight back to the airport and was making a routine landing . . . until he pushed the brake pedal. One of the wires had severed the hydraulic line to the left brake, rendering it inoperable. He used the rudder to counter the damaged brake, and they landed safely.

That collision with the power lines didn't ruffle Querns's feathers or discourage him from flying again. He graduated from his cadet course and became a fighter pilot, qualified to fly a P-47 Thunderbolt.

He was embarking on a great adventure.

★

THE AAF SENT FLIGHT OFFICER QUERNS TO A BASE IN IPSWICH, AUSTRALIA, near Brisbane. In January 1944, he and about fifteen other pilots flew there from San Francisco on a C-87 Liberator Express, a transport version of the famous B-24 Liberator bomber. The C-87 refueled at Hawaii and, as the sun went down, continued its flight.

After a few hours, flames shot out of the inner left engine. Through the windows in the fuselage, the passengers could see they were about two feet long. The pilot switched off the engine and feathered the propellers, which turned the blades sideways to reduce drag on the aircraft. After about ten minutes, the fire went out.

Querns didn't worry. The plane had three other engines.

We're still flying, he said to himself.

An hour later, the inner right engine caught fire. The flames were less intense this time and were extinguished five minutes after the pilot killed that engine and feathered the props.

But the pilot needed to take action. He decided to land the C-87 as quickly as possible. The closest airstrip was at Funafuti, a small atoll in the South Pacific. Finding Funafuti was going to be difficult because not only were they flying at night but it had started to rain.

With two engines not working, the plane was flying considerably slower. Now Querns was concerned.

How far is it to where we land this thing? he wondered. He and his fellow passengers grew quiet. The pilot didn't have to say anything to

He and his fellow passengers grew quiet.

The island was so small that the Pacific Ocean lay at *both* ends of the runway.

them. They all knew how risky it was to fly on only two engines over the Pacific at night.

The pilot alerted the Funafuti base that he was going to make an emergency landing. In response, the base sent out a Morse code radio signal to guide the plane to the atoll's landing strip. The Funafuti ground crew lit flare pots to mark the runway. The island was so small that the Pacific Ocean lay at *both* ends of the runway.

But the C-87 landed safely. Both crew and passengers were jubilant but exhausted. They stayed at Funafuti for a few days until new engines arrived from Hawaii. Then they resumed their flight to Australia.

★

QUERNS JOINED THE 39TH FIGHTER SQUADRON AND FLEW WITH THEM AT several bases as American forces moved north toward Japan.

On a sunny morning in April 1945, Lieutenant Querns and three other pilots left Clark Field, an air base near Manila in the Philippines, to attack Japanese bases on the island of Formosa, now known as Taiwan. Because of the distance to Formosa, Querns's P-47 carried an extra fuel tank. After he had used the fuel, Querns dropped the external tank. But a hose linking the main tank to the external tank didn't disconnect properly, causing a leak in the main tank.

"I'm SNAFU," Querns told the other pilots.

Querns checked his fuel gauge regularly and soon noticed that he had less fuel than expected at that point in the flight. More important, he realized that he didn't have enough to make it to Formosa and then back to Clark Field. He had to turn back.

"I'm SNAFU," Querns told the other pilots.

"Roger," one of them replied. "See you later."

Querns turned his plane around, but he was starting to fear that he might not have enough fuel to make it back to the base even from there. Was this flight his last?

He decided to fly at a lower altitude so he could set his plane down gently on the Pacific if he ran out of fuel. Then he could climb into a life raft and await rescue.

But after he had dropped down, he changed his mind. *I'm going to go to see some angels*, he thought.

Querns had ascended to about 15,000 feet when he noticed, with pleasant surprise, that the fuel gauge had stabilized. Revving the engine to fly higher somehow must have quelled the leak. He might make it— but he had a long way to go. No matter what happened, though, he wasn't going to quit.

About fifty miles away, he radioed the base to report that he was low on fuel. "I'm making a straight-in approach," he said. "I don't care who's in front of me. I'm first!"

Querns removed his radio headset so that the wires wouldn't entangle him if he had to bail.

He started his descent, reached the base, and had to make only a slight turn before landing on the runway. As he turned onto a taxiway, the engine stopped cold.

It had run out of fuel.

★

LATER THAT APRIL, QUERNS FLEW IN A GROUP OF FOUR P-51 MUSTANGS from Clark Field to Formosa again to scout enemy air bases to strafe. The pilots found one, spotted anti-aircraft guns on it, and fired at them.

When he had finished firing, he noticed a slight movement in his control stick.

What was that? he wondered.

He looked over his shoulder at the right wing and saw that the aileron—a wing flap—was missing. That was a surprise! He hadn't realized that the Japanese had fired at his plane. Apparently a flak shell had struck the aileron and knocked it off.

Time to get back to Clark Field. No need to worry, though, since the elevators—the flaps on the tail—still worked. He'd use those instead of the aileron to bring the plane down.

Even without the aileron, he landed safely.

★

SHORTLY AFTER QUERNS RETURNED TO CLARK FIELD, HIS SQUADRON moved to Mangaldan Airfield, a base about 120 miles north of Manila. But first they had to collect their aircraft.

He and seven other pilots flew as passengers on a C-47 Skytrain, the military version of the DC-3, from Mangaldan to Port Moresby, New Guinea, to pick up new P-47s and fly them back.

The P-47s, along with the C-47, left Port Moresby early in the morning. After about half an hour, the C-47 pilot, who was the flight leader, feared they might fly into heavy clouds and rain. He decided to return to Port Moresby.

Querns had flown in the area previously. The clouds were light. He wasn't worried.

"We're going to go ahead," Querns said on the radio. "Anybody want to go with me?"

Three other pilots decided to fly with him to Mangaldan.

As they flew, the weather improved. Soon there was not a cloud in the sky. After about six hours, Querns hoped to see land, but, no matter where he looked or how hard, he saw nothing except the vast expanse of the merciless Pacific.

"If you see something, let me know," he radioed to the other pilots.

No one saw anything. Nor did the planes have top-notch navigational equipment.

Querns started to feel concerned. He just wanted to see a piece of land with a runway. He adjusted his course to fly north. Surely they would find land if they kept searching.

He kept searching.

After about eight hours in the air, Querns spotted trees on the horizon. As he flew closer, he could see jungle and a landing strip. He had no idea where they were, but then he spotted something at the airstrip that gave him great relief: an American flag.

He and the three other pilots landed at the strip. The ground crew

He spotted something at the airstrip that gave him great relief.

told him that he had just landed at the naval air station at Zamboanga in the southwestern part of the Philippines.

The winds had blown Querns and the other pilots nearly 650 miles due south of their intended destination. The Zamboanga ground crew refueled the planes, and the pilots headed north to their base.

Querns was exceptionally lucky to have found the airstrip. In hindsight, he shouldn't have attempted to fly to Mangaldan without better navigation equipment.

★

AFTER 132 FLIGHTS, QUERNS RETURNED TO AMERICA IN JUNE 1945. HE graduated from Buffalo State College and then taught industrial arts at Lockport High School in his hometown. A few years later, he taught at Royalton-Hartland Central School in nearby Middleport.

Querns served with the Air Force reserves from 1945 to 1960. Then he flew helicopters as well as fixed-wing aircraft with the New York Army National Guard. When Hurricane Agnes flooded parts of New York State in 1972, he flew a National Guard helicopter to rescue residents stranded by the water, including patients at a hospital in Corning. A few years later, in 1973, his retirement from aviation duties brought tears to his eyes.

In 2011, Robert Querns holds a model of a P-47 Thunderbolt, one of the planes he flew.

But even through all the perils he faced, Querns admitted to worrying the most on board that C-87 that lost two engines. In that one instance, he had no control over the situation. Everything about that flight was uncertain. "There wasn't anything that was positive about that," he said.

Of all of his other harrowing experiences in the air, he simply said: "Never be a quitter."

DREAMING OF TROUBLE

CHARLES WARREN
Staff Sergeant
335th Squadron
95th Bomb Group
US Army Air Forces

A
S A BOY, CHARLES WARREN OFTEN WATCHED PLANES TAKE OFF and land at Fairfax Airport in Kansas City, Kansas. At age eighteen, on the afternoon of December 7, 1941, he was listening to the radio at home when the news hit the air.

"Oh crap," he said aloud, fearing that the Japanese might conquer America.

Staff at his high school advised him not to enlist immediately, noting that he would be conscripted. He waited to enlist until September 1942, when he had graduated from high school.

★

ON JANUARY 23, 1944, STAFF SERGEANT WARREN, NOW A TAIL GUNNER, had an unusual dream. God told him that he would face trouble the next day but that he would be all right. Not a particularly religious person, he discussed the dream in the morning with two of his crewmates, Staff Sergeant Frank Bialas and Staff Sergeant Andrew Torok.

"Stay on alert—extra alert—today," he told them.

Bialas and Torok appreciated the warning as they prepared to depart on a cold, foggy morning from their base at Horham in Suffolk, England. They were flying to western Germany in a B-17 nicknamed *Roarin' Bill.* Their target: the rail yard at Hucheln.

In the squadron's briefing room, Warren could see that they were going to have a difficult flight. A sheet of red cellophane covered the part of the map of Germany to which they were flying. That meant anti-aircraft guns.

On the way to Hucheln, flak flew at them. German fighters also fired at them. Shells hit the B-17, but Second Lieutenant Charles Mowers,

"We're aborting!" Mowers announced.

the pilot, kept going. About fifteen minutes before *Roarin' Bill* reached their target, flak struck the outer right engine. Smoke spewed from it. Mowers feathered the propellers to reduce wind resistance.

"Call in your post," Mowers instructed his crew over the intercom.

"Everything's fine back here," said Warren, who was shooting at German fighters from the tail. The rest of the crew was in similar shape. A few miles from the target, they opened the bomb doors, ready to release the plane's payload of 500-pound bombs. Then Mowers noticed another problem: The inner right engine was smoking as well.

"We're aborting!" Mowers announced as he turned the aircraft around to return to England. *Roarin' Bill* couldn't fly at normal speed with two malfunctioning engines, and flying slowly made the B-17 more vulnerable to attack. "Stay on alert," he added.

A strange feeling washed over Warren as he remembered his dream. Was this it? The plane had flown into trouble, but would he be all right?

"Find me an open field so I can lighten the load," Mowers said, wanting to avoid accidentally bombing civilians.

About fifteen minutes later, the crew found a spot, and Second Lieutenant Gerald Dechambre, the bombardier, released the ten bombs. The aircraft lurched upward as soon as the bombs slipped through the doors.

Nazi fighters kept firing, and the *Roarin' Bill* kept firing back. Lieutenant Ivo von Lübich-Edler Milowa, a German pilot flying a Messerschmitt 109, caught sight of the B-17 as it approached Brussels.

Flames now leapt from the two right engines.

He aimed for it and fired. A 20mm shell struck the cockpit, injuring Mowers, Dechambre, and Second Lieutenant David O'Boyle, the navigator. Flames now leapt from the two right engines.

Warren intercommed Mowers to move the aircraft to the left so he could fire at a German plane. Mowers, who had sustained a head wound, didn't respond. He wanted to give his crew as much time as possible to bail out.

"Go!" Mowers shouted to the crew near him. Several jumped through the hatch near the cockpit: Dechambre; O'Boyle; the copilot, Second Lieutenant Gerald Roderick; and the top-turret gunner, Technical Sergeant Howard Gerbert.

Warren saw the flames pouring from the two right engines. He couldn't wait any longer. He had to bail. He tried the escape door on the right side of the tail, pushing it with his feet. It didn't open. He donned his chest parachute, which had served as his seat. A piece of metal shrapnel—about an inch long and a quarter of an inch wide—had lodged in the chute. He stashed the shard in his pocket and tried the door again with his feet. Still nothing. Finally, on the third try, it flew open.

The chute was bulky, and he had to squeeze backward through the small door, so he connected only one of the parachute's two clips. As he slipped from the aircraft, the wind blew off his helmet, and flames from the engine singed the top of his head.

Bialas, the left waist gunner, helped Torok, the right waist gunner, by pulling his comrade's ripcord as he pushed him through the right

He couldn't wait any longer. He had to bail.

waist window. Bialas also helped Staff Sergeant Carlton Griffin, the radio operator, through the same window. When Bialas realized that the ball turret's hydraulic system had failed, he helped Staff Sergeant Ceber Creech, the gunner there, get out by cranking it open manually.

Everyone except the pilot bailed successfully from *Roarin' Bill*. Charles Mowers died when the plane crashed at Glabais, near Waterloo, in Belgium.

★

WARREN BAILED FROM *ROARIN' BILL* AT ABOUT NOON INTO WHAT SHOULD have been a clear, sunny day—but flak smoke had blackened the sky near the plane.

Tumbling through the air, he attached the second clip to his harness to stabilize his parachute. But he waited to pull the ripcord. If he slowed his descent too soon, he'd become a falling target for a German gunner. *Roarin' Bill* had been flying at about 27,000 feet. Warren waited until 5,000 feet to pull the cord.

That's when he noticed that the shard of shrapnel had created holes in his chute. As he drifted away from the smoke, blue sky peered down at him. He was descending faster than normal but landed safely in Court-Saint-Étienne, about twenty miles southeast of Brussels. About two hundred people at a cemetery for an interment watched as he came down, landed in a tree, and fell through it headfirst. Two girls rushed over and helped him remove his harness. One of them, Josée, a teenager, walked with him. Like many of the town's residents, she didn't speak English, so they communicated with signs. A woman who lived near the cemetery waved to them from behind the brick wall around her house on Rue Defalque, urging them to come inside. Warren pushed Josée over the wall, then followed her over.

He didn't know the woman's name, but Armande Fauconnier gave him one of her husband's suits to wear. Albert Fauconnier stood several inches shorter than the aviator, so the suit fit tightly. Madame Fauconnier gave him a pair of her husband's shoes, also too small. Then she burned Warren's uniform and ID papers in the kitchen stove, saving the tag he had worn around his neck that identified him as an American serviceman.

After about fifteen minutes, he departed and spotted a church, which he hoped would offer him sanctuary. As he walked toward it, he felt as though he was stepping into a new era.

Warren hid behind one of the pews. He didn't see any priests, but a middle-aged man, about five foot ten and two hundred pounds, soon entered the house of worship.

"*Aviateur!*" the man called out.

The man wasn't wearing a uniform, so he probably wasn't an official who could arrest him. Warren also figured that he could outrun the man if necessary.

"I'm an American," Warren said cautiously as he stood.

"Good. Come," said the man in English.

August LePoint had seen an airman parachute to the ground. He tracked him to the Fauconniers' home, where Madame Fauconnier directed him to the church. LePoint, a truck driver, was delivering newsprint to Brussels. He also belonged to the Belgian Resistance.

The soldiers dismissed his plea.

LePoint hid his passenger in the center of one of the paper rolls on his flatbed truck. He covered his ward with loose paper and pulled a tarpaulin over the cargo.

After about 150 yards, German soldiers stopped the truck to search it. Speaking in German, LePoint expressed his irritation. He had to deliver the newsprint promptly. The soldiers dismissed his plea. They removed the tarp and jabbed their bayonets down the centers of the rolls—including the one in which Warren was hiding. The Nazi soldier rustled the loose papers above his head. In that tense moment, Warren worried not about himself but about what the Germans would do to the driver. Fortunately for both, the Nazi's bayonet didn't reach far enough into the hole.

Ten long minutes later the soldiers left, and LePoint pulled the tarp back over the rolls again. After several miles, LePoint stopped and directed Warren to climb into the cab of the truck. They continued driving, but they had to stop every fifteen minutes because the truck had a coal-powered engine. Warren helped shovel coal into the burner behind the cab. LePoint referred to the Nazis as "*les Boches*" and identified himself as a member of the Resistance. He also gave Warren one of his gloves to fend off the cold.

Late that afternoon the two men arrived at LePoint's two-room apartment in Anderlecht, a Brussels suburb. LePoint's wife, Madaline, welcomed the American with open arms, and he stayed with them that night. But in the January darkness, Warren realized that he had made a terrible mistake. In his rush to leave the Fauconniers' home, he had forgotten to retrieve his identification tag. Without it, he couldn't prove he was an American flier. Without it, he couldn't defend himself from accusations of being a spy. Without it, he could be shot.

He also realized that Albert Fauconnier's name was sewn into the suit jacket he was wearing. If German agents saw the name, Fauconnier would find himself in great danger. Fortunately Fauconnier came to the same conclusion at the same time and asked LePoint to retrieve the jacket, which he did.

The next evening, LePoint took Warren to a tavern with an apartment above it. During the day, Warren stayed in the tavern, and the owners kindly gave him beer money so he looked like a regular customer. To avoid having to talk to anyone, he held a French book while sitting at a table. When the tavernkeeper's wife came to collect his tab, she spotted a glaring problem with his ruse. Distracted by the German soldiers in the tavern, Warren didn't realize that he was holding the book upside down. He set it down to pay for the beer. In silence, the owner's wife picked it up, turned it around, and handed it back, rolling her eyes at the young airman as she did so.

LePoint returned the next evening, and they went by tram to a house owned by a nurse. There, another member of the Resistance took the aviator to have his photo taken at a coin-operated photo booth. They headed out of the store with four small photos destined for false identification papers.

Shoppers had crowded the store's doorway, however, including three women in German uniforms. On the way out, Warren bumped into one of them.

He was holding the book upside down.

"Excuse me," he said, accidentally speaking in English.

"Excuse me," he said, accidentally speaking in English.

Instantly realizing his grave mistake, Warren and LePoint bolted for a moving tram, managing to return to the nurse's house without being stopped or questioned.

Back at the house, tail gunner Charles Warren became carpenter Paul Renard.

After several more days, another member of the Resistance came to escort Warren from Brussels. As plans unfolded, they learned that Field Marshal Erwin Rommel was going to drive by the apartment in a car. They asked him to kill Rommel.

"You shoot him," said a member of the Resistance. Warren looked at the pistol, a Saturday night special. It wasn't powerful enough to hit the field marshal and kill him. Warren declined.

★

ED DETROUX DIDN'T IDENTIFY HIMSELF EITHER BY NAME OR AS SECOND IN command of the Resistance in Falemprise, near the French border. But he was wearing a gray beret. Warren was told not to walk too close, but

They asked him to kill Rommel.

he made sure he could see Detroux's beret as the Belgian walked toward the Gare du Midi.

They boarded a train to Charlerois, about thirty miles south of Brussels. Warren sat near but not beside Detroux, nor did he talk to him. At Charlerois, they transferred to another train, which took them to their destination, Walcourt.

Detroux introduced Warren to the Walcourt stationmaster, Paul Coquiart, with a single word: "Charlie." Coquiart knew exactly what that meant: Charlie was the new evader.

Warren followed Coquiart to a house nearby on Rue de la Station. A man came to the door, and Coquiart repeated the word: "Charlie."

Again, no one exchanged names, but Warren entered the home of Désiré Croen, commandant of Resistance forces in the area.

Croen's wife, Jean Huart, welcomed him. *"Manger?"* she asked. Warren hadn't studied French in school, but he was learning key words quickly—and he was ready to eat.

Later that evening, Warren met another Allied evader at the house, Sergeant Alan Lucas, a Brit. The two men slept in the attic. The next day, Croen took them into the snow-covered woods near Walcourt. The Resistance used a campsite hut there to retrieve supplies dropped by the Royal Air Force.

The hut's twenty-foot walls consisted of hay bales. A holey tarpaulin served as the roof. On cold nights, the camp's denizens piled onto the bottom level of a large bunk bed and shared two blankets. Despite the rough accommodations, Warren felt comfortable. Among his twelve comrades, some came from English-speaking countries, such as Canada. Speaking English again reminded him of home, and his mind drifted to his parents. Edgar and Della Warren knew that their son was

They didn't know that the Resistance was helping him.

missing in action, but they didn't know that the Resistance was helping him or that he was going to help the Resistance.

★

AFTER A WEEK AT THE CAMP—DURING WHICH THE RAF DROPPED NO supplies—the Resistance moved Warren and Lucas to a farmhouse owned by Arthur and Julie Constant in Fontenelle, about two and a half miles away.

To escape unwanted notice, the two men stayed in the third-floor attic during the day and remained on the property at night. During their first week with the Constants, Elizabeth Neuville, another member of the Resistance, visited them. She had studied in England before the war and spoke English well. She suggested that they formulate an escape plan in case the Nazis snooped around when they came to the farm every day to pick up milk for a nearby base.

If they had to escape, Warren and Lucas decided, they would slip through the attic's back window, slide down a gutter pipe, and jump the last ten feet. Thankfully, they never had reason to put their plan into action.

As winter thawed to spring, Warren and Lucas kept abreast of the war by listening to newscasts on the Constants' radio. The BBC broadcast not only news but also coded messages for the Resistance. In the spring, the Belgian Resistance received one such message: *"Pour Oscar, la carpe est muette.*" For Oscar, the carp is silent—which meant that the Royal Air Force was going to drop supplies on the night of the next full moon, May 10.

Warren and twenty others headed into the woods that night to receive the supplies. Warren's assignment was to send a Morse code message by flashlight to the crew, telling them precisely where to drop the supplies. The dozen or so canisters that came down contained guns, ammunition, grenades, and other gear. The group separated the containers from their parachutes and hid the contents in the woods for other members of the Resistance to retrieve the next day. The work proved hard but exhilarating.

After they had finished, a member of the Resistance took the two fliers to the nearby village of Fairoul, where they stayed at the home of Abbé Evrard, a Catholic priest they knew as Ralph. From the priest's home, Warren saw Luftwaffe planes taking off and landing at the Florennes air base. Misery washed over him. He couldn't do anything to help the Allies shoot them down. He didn't know it at the time, but the pilot who had shot down *Roarin' Bill*, Lieutenant von Lübich-Edler Milowa, was based at Florennes.

At the priest's home, Warren and Lucas met two Canadian airmen, Sergeant Wilf Renner and Sergeant Norm Michie. The Canadians were staying with Maria Dardenne, another member of the Resistance. Spending time together helped dull the frustrations of their enforced idleness.

After a week with the priest, Warren and Lucas moved back to the

Misery washed over him.

Constants' home in Fontenelle. They passed the time playing hearts and the occasional practical joke. After washing Warren's shirts, Madame Constant sewed up one of the buttonholes. Warren found the perfect payback: When he saw Madame Constant's bloomers drying in the attic, he sewed up one of the legs.

Warren tried to help the Resistance however he could. He cleaned their guns, and, when he heard the abbot talk about heating the church in Fairoul, Warren resolved to help.

A slow-moving train rolled through the village each day in the late afternoon. With a couple of sacks in hand, he hopped onto the train's coal car, tossed out some coal, jumped off, and collected it. He dragged two sacks of coal a quarter of a mile to the church, bringing warmth to the parishioners—literally and figuratively.

Then, on June 6, 1944, Warren, Lucas, and the Constant family heard the news that everyone wanted to hear: The Allies had landed at Normandy. Everyone rejoiced. The invasion offered hope that the Allies would win the war. But in the meantime, Warren had to be patient.

★

ON SEPTEMBER 3, 1944, CAMILLE STAVAUX, SON-IN-LAW OF LOCAL Resistance leader Désiré Croen, arrived at the Constants' home on his motorbike.

"*L'armée est ici!*" he said. The army is here.

"*L'armée est ici!*"

For Staff Sergeant Warren, the war in Europe had ended. The flier hopped on the back of Stavaux's motorbike, and the two men sped to a nearby road, where they came across American soldiers.

"I'm an American GI," Warren said to a major. "I'm missing in action."

"How do I know who you are or what you are?" the major replied.

Warren forgot that he was wearing civilian clothes. "Man, I've been here eight months waiting for you!"

"What is it you really want?" the major asked.

"I want to go home to my mother," Warren said, adding that he also wanted some cheese, cigarettes, and candy—not just for himself but for the local Resistance fighters.

"I can give you some food," the major said.

Warren asked about the quickest way to get to Paris, where he could arrange to return home.

"The best way is the ankle express," the major said.

The Army was moving eastward to Germany, but the aviator wanted to go southwest. They couldn't help him.

After two more days with the Constants, Warren left for the City of Light on an old bicycle. He rode until it broke, then walked and hitch-hiked. At night, with farmers' permission, he slept in barns. From Paris, he flew to London, where American officers debriefed him and arranged for him to fly to an air base in Bangor, Maine.

Warren's parents still didn't know that he was alive. American forces had been moving eastward toward Germany so intently that they

"The best way is the ankle express."

Mrs. Warren had never lost faith that her son was alive.

hadn't notified the couple of their son's condition. A telephone operator on base called Kansas City. Warren's older sister, Ida Mae, answered the phone. The operator informed her that she had a collect call from Charles Warren and would she accept the charges?

"It's a what call?" Ida Mae asked before shrieking in surprise and dropping the phone.

Mrs. Warren picked up the phone. "Charlie Richard?" she asked, confirming her son's identity. Yes, Charlie Richard was calling.

Mrs. Warren had never lost faith that her son was alive.

"I'll be home soon," he told her.

He arrived in Kansas City by train in mid-September 1944 and left the Army Air Forces three months later. He intended to go to college— but he quickly changed his mind and reenlisted to help postwar Europe.

When Warren returned, serving in administrative roles, he went back to Belgium to thank those who had helped him. In some cases, he learned their real names for the first time. Madame Fauconnier returned his ID tag. She also gave him a piece of his parachute and a photo of the tree into which he fell, headfirst, when he bailed from *Roarin' Bill*.

★

STAFF SERGEANT WARREN RETURNED TO AMERICA AND CIVILIAN LIFE IN December 1948, going into the business of importing dinnerware and

In 2012, Charles Warren holds a photo of the tree into which he fell when he parachuted into Court-Saint-Étienne in Belgium.

crystal. He has returned to Belgium six times. Each time he has visited locals who helped him during the war. In 1987, he presented the town of Court-Saint-Étienne with a commemorative plaque to express his appreciation. The plaque hangs in the town hall.

He also keeps in touch with the other airmen who were with him in Belgium during the war, including regular exchanges with Wilf Renner, one of the Canadian airmen he met at the abbot's home.

The divine dream that assured him that he would survive that difficult flight on January 24, 1944, has remained as clear in his mind as ever, though Warren never again had a similar dream. He still has the shard of shrapnel, his ID tag, and the photo of the tree that Madame Fauconnier gave him.

When Warren received a piece of a cylinder from one of *Roarin' Bill*'s engines, he presented it to Mowers's family. "He gave his life," Warren reflected solemnly.

The German pilot who fired at the B-17 didn't survive the war, either. Von Lübich-Edler Milowa died on the Eastern Front.

Warren knew that he had to remain alert to stay alive. He has never forgotten that lesson from those fraught months in Belgium. "People are not alert to what happens to them every day in their lives," he said. "I watch details."

BULLDOGS OF THE AIR

FRANK BUSCHMEIER

Sergeant

350th Squadron

100th Bomb Group

US Army Air Forces

THAT DECEMBER AFTERNOON, FRANK BUSCHMEIER WENT WITH friends to a bowling alley.

"Did you hear the news?" the owner asked the boys.

They hadn't.

The owner told them about the Japanese attack on Pearl Harbor. Like so many others, Buschmeier—a senior in high school in the Terrace Park suburb of Cincinnati—hadn't ever heard of Pearl Harbor in Hawaii, a place now on everyone's lips.

Drafted into the Army in early 1943, Buschmeier applied to join the Army Air Forces, because he figured that aviation would play a significant role in the war. He was right.

★

BRIEFING OFFICERS PREDICTED THAT THE SQUADRON WOULD HAVE AN easy trip. *Miss Irish*, the B-17 named for the Irish girlfriend of a ground crew chief, was tasked with flying over German-controlled territory for only eighteen minutes. The weather report was good, the sky bright and clear. Sergeant Frank Buschmeier, the left waist gunner, climbed into *Miss Irish* on March 19, 1944, not expecting to encounter serious problems.

Taking off from Thorpe Abbotts village in Norfolk, England, Second Lieutenant John Gibbons flew *Miss Irish* to the target: a

---

Briefing officers predicted that the squadron would have an easy trip.

The explosion almost split the plane in two.

weapon-launching site at Marquise-Mimoyecques near Calais, France. They flew at about 21,500 feet. Second Lieutenant Sterling Blakeman, the bombardier, flicked the switch to release their twelve 500-pound bombs, but two remained on their racks. Technical Sergeant Ira Arnold, the upper-turret gunner and flight engineer, informed Gibbons about the bombs. They had been flying over enemy territory for just six minutes.

Sitting on an ammunition box, looking out his window on the left side of the plane, Buschmeier heard a loud, sudden whomping noise. An anti-aircraft shell had exploded in front of the plane, lifting its front section. Shrapnel hit the aircraft. Then another shell exploded near the tail. Again, shrapnel hit *Miss Irish*. Buschmeier feared the next shell would hit the aircraft dead center.

His terror was justified. The third burst struck the right side of the aircraft's radio room, blowing out a twelve-by-six-foot section of the fuse-lage. The explosion almost split the plane in two. The blast destroyed a wall between the radio room and the tail of the plane. A door landed between Buschmeier's legs. Where metal plates had formed the floor and right wall in the radio room, he saw the English Channel.

The explosion lifted Technical Sergeant Edward Walker Jr., the radio

The hole in the fuselage of Miss Irish was massive.

"The whole damn radio room is gone!"

operator, onto the radio table. Walker's badly torn legs hung over the edge of the table. Buschmeier turned to put on his parachute, but when he looked back the radio operator was gone. Walker had fallen off the table and through the hole.

Gibbons needed to know what was happening.

"Waist to pilot," Buschmeier said over the intercom. Gibbons told him to proceed. "The whole damn radio room is gone!"

Gibbons asked Arnold, the upper-turret gunner and flight engineer, to check the damage.

"He's right. The whole radio room is gone."

The tail end of *Miss Irish* shook as air rushed through the hole. The flight to France had become anything but easy. Flak had not only destroyed the radio room but also cut cables that controlled important equipment, such as the rudder. They tied the ends of the cables, which were dangling from the top of the fuselage, together so that they worked again.

Gibbons had another problem: the two bombs on the plane. If the bombs remained in their racks, they could explode when the plane landed. Gibbons instructed Blakeman and Arnold to remove the shackles that held the bombs in place. The two men released the bombs into the Channel.

Gibbons also ordered the crew to make *Miss Irish* lighter. They tossed out everything they could: guns, ammunition, even flak suits. Gibbons circled the Channel as the crew reduced the plane's weight.

Arnold, the upper-turret gunner and flight engineer, was releasing part of his twin gun setup down his turret when the ripcord of his chest parachute caught on a piece he dropped. His chute opened immediately.

He removed his harness, hoping both chute and harness would fly from the aircraft, but then the harness caught on a jagged part of the damaged plane. The crew tried, but they couldn't free it. Arnold's parachute floated out of the bomb bay, slowing the plane further.

Standing beside the waist gunner's window on the right side of the aircraft, Staff Sergeant Bernard Spragg, the ball-turret gunner, started pulling in the parachute, holding it against the exterior wall of the plane to keep it from flapping. Buschmeier relieved Spragg by holding the parachute as well. Arnold later went to the cockpit to inform Gibbons that he had lost his chute. Realizing that Arnold was despairing, Gibbons quickly solved the problem. "Here, take mine," he said, giving his parachute to the flight engineer.

Wanting to see the damage for himself, Gibbons walked to the center of the plane. He hardly believed what he saw. Buschmeier and Arnold were right: There really was no radio room.

Gibbons doubted whether he could land safely, so he suggested that everyone bail out over England. No one accepted his advice. Even though *Miss Irish* had sustained severe damage, the crew had confidence in their pilot. They trusted him. Somehow, despite the problems, Gibbons would land the plane.

As *Miss Irish* reached the English coast, Gibbons spotted a landing field. "How much farther to the base?" Gibbons asked Second Lieutenant Everett Johnson, the navigator. Johnson reported that they were fifteen minutes away.

Gibbons wasn't sure they had fifteen more minutes before the plane broke up. He decided to make an emergency landing at the airfield he had spotted.

Minutes ticked by as they flew closer. Gibbons lowered the wheels. Buschmeier sat on the floor, bracing himself. As the sun was setting, the wheels gently touched the runway, and *Miss Irish* rolled to a smooth stop. Second Lieutenant John Gibbons had made a perfect landing. Relieved, everyone scrambled from the plane.

The men at the airfield came out to see the plane, telling the crew that they had landed at an American base at Raydon in Suffolk—about thirty miles south of Thorpe Abbotts—home of the 353rd Fighter Group.

Miss Irish was in worse shape than her crew had suspected. In addition to the lost radio room, the huge hole in the fuselage, and the snapped cables, shrapnel had created more than four hundred small holes in the aircraft. The Raydon airmen were stunned. They hardly believed that a plane could fly in such condition. Without hesitation, the flight surgeon at the base prescribed the appropriate medication: scotch and gin.

The next day the crew flew back—in a different aircraft—to Thorpe Abbotts. *Miss Irish*, tough like all B-17s, had fulfilled her duty and duly became scrap metal.

★

They hardly believed that a plane could fly in such condition.

A FEW MONTHS LATER, ON JULY 29, 1944, BUSCHMEIER TOOK OFF FROM Thorpe Abbotts as the waist gunner on a flight to Germany. Gibbons had returned to America on leave, so Buschmeier was flying with a new pilot, Lieutenant William Fitzroy. This counted as the gunner's thirty-fourth mission. One more, and he too could return to the States.

Fitzroy flew his B-17, *Randie Lou*, across the North Sea to Denmark and then south to Merseburg, near Leipzig in eastern Germany, to destroy a synthetic-oil refinery. Briefing officers had predicted heavy flak, and they were right. The Germans fired anti-aircraft shells at the B-17s just before they reached the refinery. The flak hit *Randie Lou* almost immediately, but the crew discharged their payload on the target.

Minutes later, twelve Focke-Wulf 190 fighters attacked the B-17s from behind, flying through the flak from their own ground troops. At first, Buschmeier couldn't see them from the left waist gunner's position, but he heard Sergeant Joseph O'Donnell, the tail gunner, firing at them.

Buschmeier looked out his window and saw one of the fighters, but he didn't fire at it, fearing that he'd hit the tail of his own plane.

The Focke-Wulf 190s continued firing at *Randie Lou*. One shell hit the inner right engine, setting it on fire. Another struck Technical Sergeant Carmine Roberto, the radio operator, in the neck, killing him instantly. Another struck Buschmeier. It felt as if someone had punched him in the right thigh, but he held steady behind his gun. Then, as suddenly as they had appeared, the 190s vanished.

Fitzroy intercommed the crew to bail out, but Buschmeier's intercom wasn't working, so he didn't hear the order. Why was Spragg, the ball-turret gunner, walking toward him?

"Hold on!" Buschmeier said. "Where are you going?"

As they were talking, the plane curved to the left and started going down.

Spragg said that Fitzroy had given the order to bail. As they were talking, the plane curved to the left and started going down.

"Let's go!" Buschmeier said as he clipped on his parachute.

Spragg opened a door on the right side of the plane, and Buschmeier prepared to jump. Spragg booted him through the door, but Buschmeier didn't need any additional encouragement. He was more than ready to go.

As he slipped from *Randie Lou*, Buschmeier hoped his parachute would open properly. He pulled the ripcord quickly, and it did. As he floated down, Buschmeier heard the German and American planes firing at one another. The aircraft flew off, and the sky grew quiet and peaceful.

The oxygen system on *Randie Lou* had failed after sustaining damage from the Focke-Wulf 190s, so Buschmeier felt tired. He tried to rest for a few minutes as he wended his way earthward. Soon enough he was going to need all the energy he had. He landed at about noon in a tree-lined river near Naumburg, about 120 miles west of Leipzig.

Local residents, including two men wearing green uniforms, saw him descend. The men belonged to the German home guard. As they approached Buschmeier on the riverbank, they pointed machine pistols at him. A civilian in his twenties pistol-whipped Buschmeier several times as he shouted "Heil Hitler!"

Rather than dwell on the beating, Buschmeier felt thankful that he had landed safely. The home guard officers put him on the back of a motorcycle and drove him about a mile to the Naumburg town hall. There they placed him in a six-by-eight-foot cell in the basement. Several times, people opened a small metal window, pointed a pistol at him, and shouted. The Allied bombing campaign had killed thousands of Germans, both members of the armed forces and civilians.

Buschmeier feared the Germans were going to shoot him. He went to a corner of the cell so that anyone who wanted to kill him had to shoot from a difficult angle. When he checked his wound, he noticed a piece of metal. He pulled it out. A 20mm shell had embedded itself in his thigh.

After an hour and a half, a guard in a khaki uniform entered the cell. "Come."

"Where?" Buschmeier asked.

"To the hospital."

"No," Buschmeier replied. "You're not going to do that. You're going to take me into the woods and shoot me."

The man ushered Buschmeier from the cell and walked him upstairs.

On the main floor of the town hall stood a man wearing an American flying uniform.

"Who are you flying with?" the other man asked

Not knowing whether he could trust this person, Buschmeier asked the same question in return.

"I was the navigator with Fitzroy," he replied.

They had been on the same crew for such a short time that neither man recognized the other. Buschmeier told Lieutenant Floyd Hartman, the navigator, that he was a waist gunner with Fitzroy. The guard led the two men out of the building.

"They're going to take us out into the woods and shoot us."

"What are they going to do with us?" Hartman asked.

"They're going to take us out into the woods and shoot us," said Buschmeier.

As the two men walked, they spotted men in Luftwaffe uniforms who had lost limbs. Maybe the guard really was taking them to a hospital.

★

FITZROY BAILED OUT SUCCESSFULLY INTO THE GERMAN COUNTRYSIDE, but the next day, in a valley, he saw a sight that horrified him. The bodies of twelve American airmen were hanging from a log placed between two posts. German civilians had shot and hanged them. Fitzroy recognized three of the men: Lieutenant Robert Dykeman, Technical Sergeant Ira Arnold, and Technical Sergeant Floyd Douglas. They had served on his crew.

Shortly thereafter Nazi soldiers spotted and captured Fitzroy.

★

THE GUARD DID TAKE BUSCHMEIER TO A LUFTWAFFE HOSPITAL AND PUT him in a ward with a dozen German patients. As he entered, they sat up straight, a sign that they respected him as a fellow airman.

German civilians had shot and hanged them.

A doctor closed Buschmeier's leg wound with several stitches and treated it with sulfa powder to prevent infection. Buschmeier stayed in the hospital only one night.

As he was leaving the next day, he saw Spragg, the ball-turret gunner, who, like himself, had served on both *Miss Irish* and *Randie Lou*. Spragg had brought in a burned airman. He helped Buschmeier climb into the wagon that took them to the train station.

At the station, Buschmeier spotted Fitzroy. The two men nodded but didn't talk. Buschmeier didn't want the Nazis to know that he had served on Fitzroy's crew. They might use any opportunity to learn more about Allied crews. The Germans put the airmen on a train to an interrogation center at Oberursel, near Frankfurt in central Germany.

Buschmeier's interrogation session lasted only half an hour. His interrogator, a German officer, had lived in America and returned to Germany after the war broke out. Buschmeier told the officer only his name, rank, and serial number.

From Oberursel, Buschmeier went by train to a holding camp in Wetzlar, where he stayed until dispatched to a prison camp. He spent his first night in Wetzlar in a regular barracks, but on the second day his leg wound became infected, so he went to the camp hospital. He remained there for a month until his leg healed.

Buschmeier's parents, Frank and Flora Buschmeier, learned that their son was missing about a week after he parachuted from *Randie Lou*. Several weeks later, the Red Cross informed them—through the

Their son had become a prisoner of war.

Terrace Park police, who relayed the message—that their son had become a prisoner of war.

★

IN EARLY SEPTEMBER, BUSCHMEIER WENT BY TRAIN TO STALAG LUFT IV AT Gross Tychow in what is now Poland. The massive camp held thousands of prisoners in unheated huts. The men in Buschmeier's hut slept on wide bunks built for six men, three on each of two levels.

A day after he arrived, his wound became infected again. He stayed at the camp hospital for another month until it healed again.

For breakfast, the camp gave the prisoners bread, and the same for lunch. The dinner menu varied. Sometimes they ate corned beef hash; occasionally they enjoyed the luxury of sauerkraut. Red Cross parcels arrived once a month, supplementing their meager meals.

The prisoners had little to do. Life at the camp grew boring. Despite his injured leg, Buschmeier played football—one hut against another—with a ball that the Red Cross provided. He also walked the grounds, wondering when the Allies, who were gradually advancing toward Germany, would free him and the other men.

He felt lonely and regretted that he couldn't tell his parents that he was okay. He could send a letter to them each month, but the postal system worked erratically. On one occasion, seven letters mailed to him at different times arrived on the same day.

★

IN FEBRUARY 1945, THE GERMANS MARCHED BUSCHMEIER AND ABOUT ONE hundred other injured prisoners through a wooded area to the train station at Gross Tychow.

The guards gave each man half a Red Cross box and then crammed them into two boxcars not intended for passengers. Each unheated car had only a small opening for a window and no toilet facilities—only a bucket. The prisoners defended themselves against the German winter by huddling together for warmth.

The men didn't know where they were going. The Nazi government was moving them away from the advancing Soviet army, coming from the east, by shipping them to Barth, a town on the Baltic Sea, about 150 miles west of Gross Tychow.

The men sat quietly, conserving their energy.

The train stopped occasionally to give them a chance to stretch their legs. Leaving the boxcar wasn't easy for Buschmeier, and his fellow prisoners had to help him walk on the slanted gravel base of the tracks.

The trip took eight long days. Finally, the weary prisoners reached Barth and entered Stalag Luft I, which was worse than IV. The barracks were rudimentary. Buschmeier slept on the floor. For breakfast and lunch, the men still ate bread, but for dinner they had watery soup made from rehydrated vegetables and served on plates.

Life here was miserable, but the men started hearing good news. Secretly held radios revealed that Allied troops were nearing Barth. German guards confirmed the reports. Yes, despite an injured leg, little food, and dreadful living conditions, Frank Buschmeier had hope. The Allies were winning the war.

★

ON APRIL 29, COLONEL HUBERT ZEMKE, THE SENIOR AMERICAN OFFICER AT Stalag Luft I, arranged for the commander of the camp to turn it over to the Allies. Zemke suggested that the guards simply not report to the camp on May 1. The commander accepted the proposal, which avoided a confrontation. When Buschmeier awoke on May 1, no guards were standing at their usual posts.

He went into the town with some friends. There he saw a gruesome family scene: a mother, a grandmother, and several children. All had bullet holes in their heads. Buschmeier suspected the mother had killed her children, the grandmother, and herself in fear of what would happen when the Russians arrived. Russian guerrillas already were roaming around the town.

In a beautiful stone church, an American soldier played the "Colonel Bogey March" on a pipe organ. The war really was over.

★

A C-47 TRANSPORT PLANE TOOK BUSCHMEIER TO REIMS, FRANCE, AND from there he went by truck to Camp Lucky Strike, an American Army base near Le Havre. Then a B-17 flew him to a location he hadn't seen since July of the previous year: Thorpe Abbotts. The SS *Andrew Moore* sailed him from Southampton to Boston, arriving a few minutes after

All had bullet holes in their heads.

the longshoremen had finished their shift. He had to remain aboard the ship overnight. When morning came, coffee and doughnuts awaited him ashore.

At Camp Miles Standish, a nearby Army base, Buschmeier received a new uniform, money to travel to Cincinnati, and a chance to call home. But when he arrived at Union Terminal in Cincinnati, he couldn't find his parents. He asked the stationmaster if he would use the public address system to help him find them.

"I don't do that," the stationmaster said.

"You damn well better do that," Buschmeier replied, telling the man that he had done time as a prisoner of war in Germany. The stationmaster quickly changed his mind, and the Buschmeier family had a joyful reunion.

★

SHORTLY AFTER BUSCHMEIER RETURNED HOME, FITZROY, THE PILOT OF the *Randie Lou*, came to see him at Terrace Park. Fitzroy told him what happened to the three members of their crew whose bodies he saw hanging in the countryside. Buschmeier felt sick.

After the war, he became a carpenter and later an independent contractor, but he never lost his great respect for the B-17s in which he flew. They were bulldogs of the air, as were the men who flew them. In 2010, at Willow Run Airport near Detroit, he had the opportunity to fly in a B-17 operated by the Commemorative Air Force. His son Bill accompanied him, and he shared memories of his time in the skies. He never forgot how the injured Luftwaffe fliers he met in the Naumburg hospital respected him. They knew he was doing his job, just as he knew they were doing theirs.

Frank Buschmeier in 2012.

★ ★ ★

SURPRISE FLIGHT

SIDNEY RICHARD

Private First Class

87th Armored Field Artillery Battalion

P RIVATE FIRST CLASS SIDNEY RICHARD'S UNIT, BASED AT FIRST IN Banbury in Oxfordshire, England, had moved closer to the English Channel to prepare for the long-awaited Allied invasion of France. In the early evening of June 5, 1944, a captain in the 87th Armored Field Artillery Battalion approached Richard, a jeep driver for a forward-observer team with the artillery battalion, with an assignment. A regiment of the 82nd Airborne Division needed a replacement for a paratrooper who had fallen ill.

Richard had trained at Fort Benning, Georgia, as a paratrooper but had to leave the parachute program when he broke a leg on his fifth jump. His family came from French Canada, and Richard, born in Dexter, Maine, grew up speaking both English and French.

The captain didn't tell Richard—and perhaps didn't know—that the invasion started in mere hours, but Richard had become accustomed to surprises. While serving with an infantry regiment in Panama, he and several friends had been in a bar in Panama City, celebrating their return to America in two days. Military police entered the bar and ordered them back to their regiment, at Rio Hato, some ninety miles southwest. When they arrived back at base, they learned about Pearl Harbor. He wasn't going back to America anytime soon. He was twenty years old.

Richard accepted the captain's request to replace the paratrooper, eager to join the 82nd Airborne's 505th Regiment—even if

The invasion started in mere hours.

"Seventy percent of you will not come back."

temporarily—to make his sixth jump. The captain arranged for him to go immediately to an airstrip near the Channel.

★

BRIGADIER GENERAL JAMES GAVIN, COMMANDING THE 82ND AIRBORNE Division's paratroopers, spoke to his men: "Seventy percent of you will not come back," he said. But Gavin's somber prediction didn't worry Richard. That meant he had a fighting chance of surviving what lay ahead.

Coordinating the airborne division's participation proved complex. As soon as General Dwight Eisenhower, Supreme Allied Commander in Europe, launched the invasion, the 82nd Airborne Division needed 378 C-47 aircraft to fly its paratroopers to Normandy. The division's planes, along with other Allied aircraft, had black and white stripes painted on their wings and fuselage to ensure that Allied gunners could recognize them easily among countless planes careening through the sky.

On June 6, at about 2 a.m., an officer announced to Richard's platoon of thirty-six paratroopers, "Get on the plane." Richard stepped into the C-47 carrying his parachute, rations for three days, a rifle, a pistol, three ammunition belts, six grenades, and a radio. His weapons, equipment, and supplies weighed more than one hundred pounds.

Richard also had a map of his target area, Sainte-Mère-Église. It lay about five miles inland from Utah Beach, where American troops would

"Stand up! Hook up, and check your equipment!"

land later in the day. His instructions were to rendezvous with other members of the platoon, then search for German troops in or near the village and report their locations by radio to the 87th Armored Field Artillery Battalion, which would forward the information to gunners on ships in the Channel.

The aircraft took off for the hourlong trip across the Channel and flew through a sky teeming with Allied planes. The weather wasn't perfect, but the skies were less cloudy and the seas less rough than they had been the previous day. Richard thought back to his training sessions at Fort Benning. "Stand up! Hook up, and check your equipment!" "Hook up" meant connecting a cord on the parachute cover to the static line in the aircraft so that the parachute opened automatically. "Check your equipment" meant inspecting the equipment on the man ahead.

The pilot slowed the C-47 to about ninety miles an hour and descended to about 450 feet to reduce the opportunity for German gunners to fire at the paratroopers. "Stand up! Hook up, and check your equipment!" came the order. Richard leapt out of the aircraft and floated through the dark night into enemy territory.

Richard leapt out of the aircraft and floated through the dark night into enemy territory.

He landed on a small farm on the outskirts of Sainte-Mère-Église. Two other members of the 505th Regiment should have landed near him, but he couldn't see them. He did see a young woman carrying a milk can from a barn to the farmhouse, however.

"*Je suis un Américain,*" he said to her. I'm an American.

"*Je sais,*" she replied. I know.

She expressed her happiness that the Americans had arrived, but he didn't ask about Germans in the area. Better to observe the surroundings before he asked probing questions.

He wandered the quiet countryside, relieved to be alive. After half an hour, death reared its head: He came across the bullet-ridden body of a German soldier. Later, in a hedge, he spotted a German soldier holding a rifle. Richard pulled his pistol before he realized that the soldier was dead. The Allied troops who had shot and killed him had propped up his body.

In the night, the sounds of war slowly replaced the rustic silence into which he had fallen. A bombardment was taking place as planes flew over Sainte-Mère-Église. Other members of the 505th Regiment were fighting German forces.

One soldier's experience became legendary. The parachute of Private John Steele had caught on the steeple of the village church. With an injured leg, Steele tried to free himself but failed. After two fruitless hours, two German soldiers, Rudolf May and Alfons Jackl, helped him

The sounds of war slowly replaced the rustic silence into which he had fallen.

Within seconds, a deadly shell
sailed through the overcast sky.

down and took him prisoner. He later escaped, rejoined the Allies, and was transferred to a hospital in England. Richard and others soon heard about Steele's strange fate on the church's steeple.

Shortly before dawn, the Germans evacuated Sainte-Mère-Église. The Allies had liberated the village.

Richard met up with paratroopers from the 505th, and together they canvassed local residents, who knew Germans were in the area— but not precisely where. About 9 a.m., they spotted Nazi troops. He carefully radioed the 87th Armored Field Artillery. Within seconds, a deadly shell sailed through the overcast sky and exploded near its target. Throughout the day and into the night, the paratroopers sought out Germans and reported their positions. If the initial shells didn't hit their targets, Richard supplied additional intel, advising the gunners to aim up or down, left or right. When a shell landed right on target, he told them to "fire for effect"—and they did. The paratroopers moved east, hedge by hedge, farm by farm.

Thousands of Allied troops poured into Normandy. Within a few days, the 82nd Airborne Division released Richard from his temporary position. He rejoined the 87th Armored Field Artillery Battalion as a gunner.

★

They came face-to-face with five German soldiers aiming rifles at them.

THE ARTILLERY BATTALION ALSO MOVED EAST. BY SEPTEMBER IT HAD reached the village of Dangers, about fifty miles southwest of Paris. There Richard and two members of his battalion entered a vacant chateau, hoping to find some forgotten bottles of wine and have a pleasant evening. Instead, they came face-to-face with five German soldiers aiming rifles at them.

The three Americans immediately surrendered and handed their rifles to the Germans, but a short time later the Germans heard the sound of trucks and tanks outside. One went to investigate the commotion. When he returned, the Nazi soldiers spoke among themselves for a few minutes. Then they gave Richard and his comrades their rifles back before turning over their own. The Allies had just liberated Dangers. The five Germans wisely countersurrendered while they still had the chance.

★

THE 87TH ARMORED MOVED TOWARD PARIS BUT NOT INTO THE CITY proper. The Allies wanted the French Resistance to liberate the city, which they did. The battalion bypassed Paris and, in early December, went north toward Belgium. There Richard joined an armored cavalry unit as a forward observer.

The Wehrmacht had launched a counteroffensive in France,

Belgium, and Luxembourg soon to become known as the Battle of the Bulge. In the confusion and chaos, Richard became separated from his armored unit and decided to return to Trois-Ponts, the town in eastern Belgium that he recently had left. The wife and daughter of the town's mayor—whom the Germans had arrested—gave him information about Germans in the area.

As he was telling them why he had returned, they heard troops outside and instantly fell silent. They cracked open a door to find German soldiers marching down the street—then darted back inside.

The mayor's wife feared that the Germans would kill them all.

"Nous vous cachons," she said as she looked for civilian clothes for him to wear. We'll hide you. The two-story home had several bedrooms, and the property had a small farm with a barn and a few cows. Richard passed the time either in his bedroom or working on the farm. Yet another surprise came when he entered the house the next day to discover a German officer in the mayor's home office. Keeping his cool and his silence, Richard went about his chores around the property.

An assistant to the mayor introduced Richard to a member of the Belgian Resistance, who invited him to help place grenades in areas where German troops walked. It paled in comparison to leaping head-long from a plane, but it was more exciting than mucking out cow stalls. The Resistance set up the grenades to explode when a German soldier tripped a wire—although sometimes they exploded soon after being placed.

"Nous vous cachons." We'll hide you.

Richard had been at the mayor's house for more than a week when a Yugoslavian who had been fighting with the Germans turned himself in to the mayor's assistant. The man spoke only broken French, but clearly he wanted to surrender. The assistant suggested that Richard escort the soldier to the American troops who had arrived on the other side of the River Salm, which flowed through Trois-Ponts.

Richard accepted the mission. The Yugoslavian knew nothing about Richard except that he would take him to the Americans. The two men headed away from the village before crossing the river, a tributary of the Meuse. They walked where it ran shallow and swam where it ran deep. Richard carried his uniform in a bundle tied to a stick that he held above him as he swam through the frigid December water that reminded him of the rivers in winter back home.

After they crossed, the two men dressed. Richard donned his American uniform, which surprised and scared the Yugoslav. Richard tried to assure him that he was safe.

They walked down a road for half a mile and came upon two American soldiers.

"*Halt!*" one of them yelled. "Who's there?"

"I'm an American," Richard replied.

"What's the password?"

"I don't know," said Richard, flummoxed. But he identified himself as a member of the 87th Armored Field Artillery Battalion. The Yugoslav immediately surrendered.

The two soldiers took Richard to an officer, who questioned him. The officer immediately sent him by truck to an American base at Liège. Officers there interrogated him, and within two days—after he told them his story and showed them his identification tag—he rejoined his

Sidney Richard with his collection of medals in 2012.

battalion. The Battle of the Bulge came to an end as the Allies regained the offensive in early 1945. Week by week, they pushed deeper into Germany. The Nazi government surrendered on May 8, 1945. The war in Europe had ended.

★

AFTER THE WAR, RICHARD RETURNED TO CIVILIAN LIFE, BUT AFTER THREE months he rejoined the Army and served with the American occupational force in Germany. Later, in Korea, he jumped with the 187th Regimental Airborne Combat Team.

He retired from the Army in 1962 and worked for Sears, Roebuck and Company, but he never forgot what he had learned from his ordeals, particularly on the eve of D-Day, when he unexpectedly became a paratrooper again: "Pay attention to what you learn and remember it."

Sidney Richard died in 2012 at the age of ninety-one.

★ ★ ★

REMEMBERING A FRIEND

ALLEN JONES
577th Squadron
392nd Bomb Group
US Army Air Forces

O N SATURDAY, DECEMBER 6, 1941, ALLEN JONES HEARD GENE Tunney, the famous heavyweight boxer, predict in a speech at Northwestern University that America would join World War II within three weeks. Isolationist students in the audience booed Tunney. Jones, a history major there, was not of their number. The Japanese government had become so belligerent that Tunney's time span seemed more than realistic.

The next day, Jones walked into the Phi Gamma Delta fraternity house and noticed several students listening intently to a radio in the living room.

"What's up, everybody?" he asked.

"*Shhh*," the students replied.

Tunney's prediction had come true more quickly than either he or Jones had imagined.

Jones's friend and fellow Northwestern student Ensign Harold Christopher was serving on the USS *Nevada*. When Jones learned that Christopher had died in the attack, he enlisted in the Army Air Forces. By ending American lives, Pearl Harbor also ended the isolationist movement. Virtually everyone now wanted to help the Allies defeat Germany and Japan.

★

ON JUNE 21, 1944, SECOND LIEUTENANT ALLEN JONES WAS SERVING AS THE navigator of a B-24 Liberator known as the *Axis Grinder* in the 577th

Isolationist students in the audience booed.

Sekul found Jones on the floor.

Squadron of the 392nd Bomb Group, based at Wendling in East Anglia, England. At about four a.m., First Lieutenant Hans Belitz, Jones's pilot—an American who had emigrated from Germany at age thirteen—took off into a clear sky. Their target: a military factory at Genshagen, a suburb of Berlin.

En route, Belitz called Jones on the intercom, but Jones didn't respond. Concerned, Belitz asked Staff Sergeant John Sekul, the flight engineer and upper-turret gunner, to find out why. Sekul found Jones on the floor. Guessing that the oxygen system might have malfunctioned, Sekul connected a container of oxygen to Jones's mask, which revived him. Belitz feared the oxygen system might malfunction again and decided to return to base. The *Axis Grinder* was about eighty miles from Genshagen, but the crew jettisoned their bombs and Belitz dropped to 12,000 feet, an altitude at which they could breathe without worrying about the oxygen system.

Two Messerschmitt 109 fighters suddenly appeared and fired, breaking the Plexiglas in the nose turret, which struck Staff Sergeant William Smith, the nose gunner, in the face. Jones went to help Smith. He used all his strength to open the turret. Dazed, Smith was bleeding profusely. Jones dragged him from the turret and up the steps to the flight deck, leaving the nose gunner there to rest. Sekul also had sustained head wounds, but they weren't as serious as Smith's.

Smith was bleeding profusely.

While Jones was helping Smith, Staff Sergeant Harry Walz, the tail gunner, saw flak shells exploding near the plane. With no clouds to use as cover to hide from German pilots and flak gunners, Belitz dropped to 120 feet. As the *Axis Grinder* dived, Jones gripped the navigator's table and gave the pilot directions from their position in northern Germany back to Wendling.

"We're guzzling a lot of fuel," Belitz warned on the intercom. He didn't think they had enough to make it back.

The *Axis Grinder* flew just above the trees for half an hour. Walz, the tail gunner, spotted a freight train with a flak gun and fired at it. As they flew over a Luftwaffe base, gunners fired at the plane. The flak sounded like gravel shaking in a tin can. It exploded a box containing ammunition, which hit Staff Sergeant Bradford Vineall, one of the waist gunners, and broke his arm. The flak also hit both right engines, damaging the outer one and starting a fire in the inner one. The aircraft dropped so low that the propellers on the outer left engine hit a chimney and fell off. Jones watched them roll along the ground beneath them. The *Axis Grinder* was flying on only one engine.

Then the aircraft hit trees. A branch pierced the plane and struck Jones in the right leg so hard that he feared his leg had broken.

"We're not going to be able to reach the Channel!" Belitz said on the intercom. "We're going to set it down. Get back on the flight deck!"

The aircraft dropped so low that the propellers on the outer left engine hit a chimney and fell off.

Jones sat with his back to the fuselage and braced for impact—but the plane landed smoothly in a field of rye near the town of Aldrup in northwest Germany. The crew jumped out and the copilot, Second Lieutenant Robert Loar, rushed into the five-foot-high rye and hid.

★

GERMAN CIVILIANS WHO LIVED NEAR THE CRASH SITE CAME TO SEE THE B-24. Belitz reported that his crew needed medical assistance. Three Luftwaffe officers quickly arrived and approached with guns drawn. They frisked the Americans and took Belitz's handgun.

They piled everyone—except Loar, still hiding—into a truck and drove to a farmhouse, where Belitz gave Jones an injection of morphine from the plane's first aid kit. After the sun had set, Loar began walking west, hoping to escape Germany on foot.

A doctor from the Luftwaffe base arrived at the farm, but so did two members of the notorious Schutzstaffel, who wanted custody of the airmen. Fortunately for the crew, the doctor was a colonel and outranked the SS men, which meant he had the authority to overrule their demand. The doctor kept the crew under the Luftwaffe's more humane control. Jones's leg was badly bruised, not broken, but he sent Smith to a hospital anyway.

The Luftwaffe separated the officers from the enlisted men and took the officers, Jones and Belitz, to the base. During the night, guards woke the two men and took them to the train station at Osnabrück, where they rejoined the other members of the crew except for Smith, who remained at the hospital, and Loar, who had escaped.

While Jones and his six crewmates waited for a train, an air-raid

An air-raid siren started wailing.

siren started wailing. Allied aircraft bombed the rail yard. The two guards locked the airmen in a closet usually reserved for storing fish and ran to a bomb shelter. Jones feared that one of the bombs would hit the station, but thankfully they all missed.

After the air raid, the Luftwaffe guards released the airmen, and they boarded a train to Frankfurt. The station's roof had been destroyed during the bombing raid, as had a nearby neighborhood.

"Military objective," one of the guards cracked as he pointed to shattered civilian buildings.

"Coventry, too," Belitz replied, referring to the English city that the Luftwaffe had nearly destroyed in 1940. The guard didn't respond.

The Luftwaffe guards took the crew by streetcar to the Dulag Luft interrogation center in Oberursel. Jones spent a day in solitary confinement. The next day, he met an interrogation officer, who shook his hand and wanted to know what had happened to the missing members of the crew. He didn't know about Loar or that the crew of the *Axis Grinder* didn't need a separate bombardier. Jones served as both navigator and a bombardier. He gave only his name, rank, and serial number.

The interrogation officer tried to intimidate him: "You heard of the Gestapo?"

"You heard of the Gestapo?"

"Allen Jones, second lieutenant, serial number 0747589."

From the interrogation center, Jones and Belitz went to a camp at Wetzlar, where Jones received supplies such as a razor and a coat. He also gave the Red Cross information it needed to inform his parents that he was alive and had become a prisoner of war.

From Wetzlar, Jones and Belitz were sent by train to Sagan, about one hundred miles southeast of Berlin, where the Luftwaffe operated Stalag Luft III, a prison camp. They arrived on June 26, five days after landing in the field of rye.

On the day Jones arrived at Stalag Luft III's south compound, Lieutenant Colonel Albert Clark, head of security there, talked to him about the challenges of escaping. Clark advised him that, unless he spoke German, the odds of a successful escape looked slim. Clark knew that the Germans had executed fifty Allied prisoners whom they had recaptured after escaping—the escape that inspired Paul Brickhill's *The Great Escape*.

For the few days after Jones arrived, no one talked of escaping, but First Lieutenant Joe Consolmagno organized a celebration for Independence Day. He arranged for a major to tell everyone early in the morning on the Fourth of July to "Get up!" and warn that "The Redcoats are coming." Once awake, the prisoners found that Consolmagno had planned athletic events for them. He even organized swimming contests in the pools of water used to extinguish fires. The guards let their American prisoners celebrate Independence Day. Most of the prisoners

"Get up! The Redcoats are coming."

decided not to attempt escape, but a few did. During the next winter, two prisoners planned to use wire cutters to go through the fences just before the 4 p.m. roll call. They asked Jones to distract the guards with a snowball fight. The two prisoners escaped, but were caught a few hours later.

The prisoners read books supplied by the Swedish YMCA. They dreamed of going home, but they also knew that the Nazi government wanted its army, navy, and air force to fight for as long as possible. Nor did the Allies have any intention of negotiating with the Third Reich; they demanded nothing less than unconditional surrender.

★

ON JANUARY 27, 1945, MAJOR JAMES O'BRIEN, A BLOCK COMMANDER AT THE compound, warned the men to be ready to leave in half an hour. The prisoners didn't know where they were going, but Jones and other men suspected that the Germans might move them away from the Soviet forces invading Germany from the east.

The prisoners took extra clothing and food, such as chocolate bars, from their Red Cross boxes. Jones carried his supplies in a blanket slung over his shoulder. The men left the compound at 11 p.m. and marched through the countryside until 6 a.m., when they stopped at a farm. They stayed there until 6 p.m., then marched until 3 a.m. On January 29, they reached a tile factory at Muskau. With two thousand prisoners in the building, space was so limited that Jones started to climb into a metal container to sleep, but he was so exhausted that he passed out in the process. His comrades caught the container before it fell over, and Jones found a place on the floor.

Mile after mile, one foot in front of the other, one foot in front of the other.

Colonel Charles Goodrich, senior American officer at the south compound, told the Germans that his men would go no farther without rest. The Germans permitted the men to stay at the tile factory until 7 a.m. on January 30.

Mile after mile, one foot in front of the other, one foot in front of the other. Jones refused to think about lying down in the snow because he might never get up again.

Finally, around midafternoon on the thirtieth, the men reached Spremberg, where they ate hot barley soup outside a German army base. It was their first real meal since leaving Stalag Luft III. But they weren't allowed inside the building.

Later that afternoon, Jones and the other prisoners boarded boxcars at a train station. The men remained in those cars for two days and two nights without toilets or even buckets. The train eventually stopped at Moosburg, about thirty miles northeast of Munich. The massive prison camp there, Stalag VII-A, had a lice infestation and miserable conditions. Many prisoners became ill. Jones managed to remain reasonably healthy, except for a mild case of dysentery. He reunited with Sekul, the flight engineer and upper-turret gunner. Walz, the tail gunner, and Loar, the copilot—both eventually captured—were there, too.

So was Belitz. He had exchanged identification tags with an enlisted man and went to a different barracks. Under the Geneva Convention, enlisted men were permitted to work. He had hoped that would give him

A tank from General George Patton's Third Army crashed through the gate.

a chance to escape. He was assigned to remove debris at a marshaling yard in Munich and jumped on a passing train. He traveled west until he met American troops and eventually returned to America.

For Second Lieutenant Allen Jones, the war ended on April 29, 1945. Only a small contingent of guards reported for work. Later that day, a tank from General George Patton's Third Army crashed through the gate. Everyone was free. Everyone rejoiced.

A civilian on a jeep asked whether anyone was from Illinois, Michigan, Indiana, or Wisconsin. A reporter with the *Chicago Tribune*, he was writing a story about men at the camp who hailed from those four states. Jones gave his name and address in Michigan. His girl-friend, Lynn Skelton, later saw the story and knew that her boyfriend had survived and was free.

When the war in Europe ended in May, Jones flew from Moosburg to Regensburg, in southeast Germany, and from there to Camp Lucky Strike, an American base near the French harbor city of Le Havre. He sailed to Hoboken, New Jersey, on the *Thomas H. Barry*, an Army troop-ship. Then he rode a train to Grand Haven, Michigan, where his parents brought him home to Fruitport. The Army Air Forces released him in September, and in December he and Lynn married.

★

Allen Jones in 2011.

JONES EARNED HIS MASTER'S DEGREE IN POLITICAL SCIENCE FROM Columbia University and worked in furniture manufacturing in Chicago, moving later to Louisville, Kentucky.

In 1995, he returned to Germany with several busloads of former prisoners to visit some of the places he had experienced during the war. At Spremberg, Jones saw the army building where he and the other prisoners had eaten barley soup in the cold outside. In the postwar years, it had become a municipal building, and the visitors enjoyed a dinner provided by the city. The menu included barley soup and also—not on the menu in 1945—beer.

Thinking back to his fateful flight on the *Axis Grinder*, Jones remembered that he was concerned but never afraid. Every year on Memorial Day, he thinks first not about the hardships that he endured but about Harold Christopher, his friend from Northwestern who was killed on the *Nevada*.

★ ★ ★

SIX CREWMATES

JOHN RAISER
Second Lieutenant
732nd Squadron
453rd Bomb Group
US Army Air Forces

G ROWING UP IN GLENSIDE, PENNSYLVANIA, JOHN RAISER SHOWED an early interest in aviation. He loved visiting nearby Pitcairn Field to watch the aircraft. At age eight, he went for a ride on an autogiro, an early type of helicopter. As a teenager, he took flying lessons. On December 7, 1941, he was seventeen years old and working in the packing department of a Philadelphia steel company. As soon as he turned eighteen, he enlisted in the Army Air Forces. He wanted to fly.

★

IN THE EVENING OF JUNE 23, 1944, SECOND LIEUTENANT RAISER WAS flying his B-24 bomber back to base at Old Buckenham in England after he and his crew had bombed a German air base near Reims in northern France. The Germans had fired anti-aircraft shells, but his aircraft— *Begin the Beguine*, after the Cole Porter song—escaped damage.

Raiser was flying at 22,000 feet over the Netherlands when flak from German anti-aircraft guns hit another plane in his formation, damaging its oxygen system and forcing it to a lower altitude. Raiser wanted to stay near the other bomber, so he descended with it to 17,500 feet. The lower altitude helped the crew on the damaged aircraft, but it made the *Begin the Beguine* an easier target.

A shell struck the left wing of the aircraft so powerfully that it lifted the bomber. Something—a piece of metal, perhaps—tore through Raiser's upper right triceps, rendering him incapable of pushing the throttle levers.

He prayed and thought of his parents.

He didn't have time to alert the crew on the intercom and tell them

Then the bomber exploded.

to bail. He wasn't sure what the fastest way out of the aircraft was, but he considered the bomb bay doors. He was wearing his parachute already. He removed his helmet and oxygen mask with his left arm.

Then the bomber exploded. The explosion blew out the armor plate beside him on the left side of the cockpit. Daylight poured through the two-foot hole.

Raiser unbuckled his seat belt and signaled to his copilot, Second Lieutenant John Gentile, that he was bailing. When he was partly through the hole, his boots snagged on jagged metal. Opening his parachute would pull him from the plane, but the chute might catch on the tail wing. He looked back and saw the plane's tail spiraling earthward.

Raiser found the strength in his injured arm to pull the ripcord. The chute opened, yanking him out of his boots. He wasn't going to catch on the tail wing, but he still feared hitting one of the propellers. But the left side of the plane didn't have any propellers anymore. The explosion had sheared off the entire left wing.

One of his parachute seams ripped as the chute opened, plummeting him earthward. He saw one member of his crew safely parachuting and prayed to see more. Moments later, another chute. As

He looked back and saw the plane's tail spiraling earthward.

If the Germans found him with a gun, they might use it on him.

Raiser came down near the city of Vlissingen on the Dutch coast, white streaks from tracer bullets whizzed past in the dark. They came from German machine guns, but none hit him.

Raiser made out that he was going to overshoot Vlissingen and land in the North Sea. He had to slip out of his parachute so it wouldn't drag him underwater. He loosened one of the harness buckles before impact. The cold seawater shocked his system, but it also slowed the flow of blood from his wound.

A stiff sea breeze pulled at his half-open parachute, dragging Raiser away from the coast toward an anti-submarine net. He held on to the net, releasing the remaining buckles on his harness and dropping a box containing his escape equipment and his handgun into the sea. If the Germans found him with a gun, they might use it on him.

He was about a quarter of a mile from a harbor, and a German navy crew was inflating a yellow rubber dinghy. He had been floating in the water for about half an hour when the dinghy arrived.

"Für Sie ist der Krieg vorbei," one of the crew told him. He knew what the words meant. For you the war is over. He also knew what lay ahead. He was twenty years old and now a prisoner of war.

The crew pulled him from the water and transferred him to a motor launch. He was shaking. A medic cut open his right sleeve to examine his injured arm. He saw bone. Onshore, another medic spread sulfa powder on the wound and gave him an injection. He soon stopped shaking.

A medic cut open his right sleeve to examine his injured arm. He saw bone.

German guards drove him to Rotterdam. On the way, they picked up Raiser's copilot, Gentile. The guards didn't permit the two men to speak to each other, but Raiser delighted at seeing his crewmate. At Rotterdam, the two airmen were taken to a hospital. Dutchmen walking in the street spotted the two airmen and, realizing they were captured Americans, saluted and made the "V" for victory sign. The German guards pointed their guns at the Dutchmen but held their fire.

At the hospital, the Germans treated Raiser's wounded arm and told him they had found the fuselage of his plane. There were "*sechs tote.*" Six dead. The number seared itself into his mind. Everyone on board had died except him, Gentile, and the other crewman he had seen parachuting down.

The next day, the guards took him from the hospital to solitary confinement. A few days later, he was taken to a train station, where he came across his bombardier, Second Lieutenant Art Foreman—the other airman he had seen.

Foreman had sustained serious injuries. Bandages covered his entire head except for his nose and lips. Foreman asked for water. The guards allowed Raiser to lead Foreman to a water fountain. A woman ahead of them turned around, saw Foreman, and fainted.

Foreman described how he had left their aircraft through a hole created when the nose wheel blew off. He had tried to help Staff Sergeant Robert Neily from the nose turret, but Neily had been trapped. After he

He put his hand to his hair and realized that he was on fire.

bailed, Foreman smelled something burning. He put his hand to his hair and realized that he was on fire.

Gentile, the copilot, was also at the station and also injured. A piece of flak had struck his left buttock.

The three men went by train to Frankfurt. Guards put them in a compartment with the blinds drawn so they couldn't see the damage that Allied bombers had done. At the Frankfurt station, a guard advised the three men not to escape. Civilians, angry at the bombing of their city, were prepared to kill Allied airmen. The roof was still on the station, but all the surrounding buildings had been destroyed. The guards drove the three airmen to Dulag Luft, an interrogation center near Frankfurt, where the men went into solitary.

★

THE NEXT DAY, GUARDS TOOK RAISER TO AN INTERROGATION OFFICER, who introduced himself as a major. He spoke perfect English and politely offered his charge a cigarette. Raiser declined.

The interrogator knew a surprising amount about the bomb group. He knew the name of the 453rd Bomb Group's commanding officer, Colonel Ramsay Potts, and that Jimmy Stewart, the actor, served as its operations officer. Raiser had had lunch with Stewart back at their base.

"We can easily add your name to your dead crew," the interrogator warned.

"All we want to know is your bomb load and your target," the major said.

Raiser followed orders and gave only his name, rank, and serial number—not knowing that his rank was out of date. That day the US Army Air Forces had promoted him from second lieutenant to first lieutenant.

"We can easily add your name to your dead crew," the interrogator warned, pointing out that Germany had not notified the Red Cross about any survivors. A guard placed a rifle to Raiser's head.

Raiser prayed but also assumed that the major didn't want brains all over his office, so he continued to give the same information:

"John Raiser, second lieutenant, 0692819."

Raiser's hunch was right. The interrogator sent him back to his cell. The next day, he went by train to Stalag Luft III, the prison camp for Allied air force officers at Sagan in eastern Germany.

On the way to Sagan, the train stopped at a Red Cross camp, which provided the men with food and clothing. Medical staff there changed the bandage on Raiser's arm.

When Raiser arrived at the camp on July 2, officials placed him in Center Compound with about two thousand other American prisoners. He quickly acclimated to the routine. He woke up, lined up outside for the head count, ate breakfast, and then went to the camp hospital, where a British or American doctor treated his arm.

A few days after arriving, he started recording his experiences in a blue notebook provided by the Red Cross. He dedicated the second page to the six members of his crew who didn't survive the downing of the *Begin the Beguine*. Under six crosses, he listed their names: Technical Sergeant Lonnie O. Morris, from Texas; Technical Sergeant Joseph F. Sills, from Pennsylvania; Staff Sergeant Alfred W. Larson, also from Pennsylvania; Staff Sergeant George S. Layman, from Oklahoma; Staff Sergeant Quinto B. Vittori, from Michigan; and Staff Sergeant Robert W. Neily from California.

Raiser's parents knew nothing about their son's ill-fated flight until three days after he arrived at Stalag Luft III. They received a telegram on July 5 declaring him missing in action. On July 18, a second telegram informed them that the International Red Cross had reported that he was a prisoner of war.

Three months later he received his first letter from home. With help from the Red Cross, prisoners could send four cards and two letters a month. They also received Red Cross parcels, which enabled them to supplement the camp's meager rations.

Even after the Gestapo captured and shot fifty of the seventy-six men who escaped, two prisoners tried to escape from Raiser's compound by swinging along overhead electrical wires. They wore insulated gloves to avoid electrocuting themselves, but the wires crossed and sparked. The men had to drop to the ground as guards switched on searchlights. The pair raced back to their barracks and managed to avoid further detection.

To pass the time, Raiser listened to Peggy Lee's "St. Louis Blues" over and over. He closed his eyes, and for a short time the music took him back home. He also studied Spanish—in case he managed to get to Spain, a neutral country—and celestial navigation. But he never had the chance to put his knowledge to the test. Any hope of a quick return home ended when the Nazis launched the Battle of the Bulge.

★

HITLER HAD LONG PLANNED TO MOVE PRISONERS OF WAR AWAY FROM THE advancing Allied armies. At the end of January 1945, Soviet forces were nearing Sagan. On the evening of January 27, guards warned the prisoners in Center Compound to prepare to march through the countryside.

Raiser partnered up with a roommate, Second Lieutenant Nick Ursiak, the copilot of a B-17 shot down at Quakenbrück in northwest Germany in October 1943. Ursiak had been studying German, and together the pair made a supply sled by turning a wooden bench upside down and attaching a rope to it. They loaded it with sweaters, raisins, and chocolate bars. Raiser stuffed his blue notebook inside his shirt, close to his chest.

The prisoners left the compound at 5:30 a.m. the next day. Snow fell, and the temperature dropped to 8 degrees. The exhausted men rested at churches, a factory, and a barn. In Muskau, where the men rested at a brick factory, Raiser spoke to a maintenance man, who showed him a photo of his son, a prisoner of war in Pennsylvania. The young German had *gained* thirty-five pounds in prison.

After a few days, the temperature rose. When the snow melted, Raiser and Ursiak couldn't pull their sled over the bare ground, so they discarded it, along with anything they couldn't carry.

On February 4, the prisoners arrived at the Spremberg train station.

They used the toilet seats for firewood.

Guards herded them into boxcars designed for cattle. With sixty men to a car but no toilets, the men relieved themselves on the ground whenever the train stopped. At one point, Raiser noticed a guard with his rifle slung over his shoulder, talking to a prisoner. Raiser had bought a knife from another guard for ten cigarettes. He used it clandestinely to remove the rubber stopper at the end of the first guard's rifle barrel and then poured sand down the rifle.

On February 7, the train car arrived at Stalag VII-A near Moosburg in southern Bavaria. The prisoners had little food and no hot water or facilities in which to bathe. They used the toilet seats for firewood. After two weeks, some of the prisoners went on strike and refused to cooperate until conditions improved. The tactic worked. Within days, Raiser was able to take a shower.

Despite the conditions, the prisoners knew the Allies were winning the war. By mid-April, the Germans couldn't maintain the camp's physical structure. Prisoners removed some of the fences separating the compounds and roamed the grounds freely. Raiser reconnected with Art Foreman, his burned bombardier from the *Begin the Beguine*. German doctors had operated on him to treat his burns.

On April 29, tanks from General Patton's Third Army rolled into the camp. Two days later, Patton himself arrived, wearing his silver helmet and carrying two ivory-handled pistols. Standing on a jeep, he told the men to report any guards who had abused them.

> ## Patton himself arrived, wearing his silver helmet and carrying two ivory-handled pistols.

★

A FEW DAYS LATER, RAISER WAS DRIVEN BY TRUCK TO STRAUBING AIRPORT and flew to Le Havre. On May 19, he boarded the USS *General W. H. Gordon* and sailed into New York City. On June 3, they beheld the Statue of Liberty and wept. Fireboats celebrated their safe arrival by spraying jets of water into the air.

The two members of Raiser's crew who bailed from the *Begin the Beguine*, John Gentile and Art Foreman, both returned to the States. Foreman attended medical school and practiced medicine in California. Gentile worked for General Electric in Springfield, Massachusetts. Nick Ursiak, Raiser's march partner from Stalag Luft III to Spremberg, went to work at Pittsburgh Plate Glass Company (later known as PPG Industries).

John Raiser remained in the US Army Air Forces for several more months, then worked in his father's grocery store. Later, he moved to

> ## They beheld the Statue of Liberty and wept.

Raleigh, North Carolina, where he owned a kitchen design company. He retired to Florida, first to Tiger Point, then Pensacola. He died in 2011 at the age of eighty-seven, no doubt thinking to the very end about Larson, Layman, Morris, Neily, Sills, and Vittori—his six crewmates who weren't as fortunate as he was.

★ ★ ★

SOFT LANDING

ROBERT POWELL
Second Lieutenant
328th Squadron
352nd Fighter Group
US Army Air Forces

A S A YOUNG BOY, BOB POWELL FOUND FLYING FASCINATING. HE made toy airplanes from anything he could find, even old window slats. In 1927, the year that Charles Lindbergh flew across the Atlantic, his father took him to an airfield, where he met a World War I pilot who offered biplane rides for two dollars. That was a lot of money at the time, but Powell persuaded his dad to buy him a ticket.

Years later, while studying journalism at West Virginia University in Morgantown and after the Japanese attacked Pearl Harbor, Powell developed a different interest in aviation. His roommate and child-hood friend, Earl Ashworth, persuaded him to hitchhike with him to Pikeville, Kentucky, to take the Army Air Forces exam to qualify for pilot training. "Punchy" Powell—so called because he was a Golden Gloves boxing champ in high school—passed, but Ashworth failed. (He tried again a month later and passed.)

West Virginia University offered full course credit to students who enlisted. Powell took advantage of that offer, and Second Lieutenant Bob Powell became a fighter pilot, serving with the 328th Squadron of the 352nd Fighter Group, based at Bodney in Norfolk, England.

★

ON JULY 18, 1944, POWELL SAT IN THE COCKPIT OF A P-51 MUSTANG FIGHTER he had named *The West "by Gawd" Virginian*. The phrase came from West Virginia mountaineers, who often had to explain that West Virginia isn't part of Virginia. He and forty-seven other pilots lined up in flights of four, ready to escort bombers coming home from the conti-nent. By now, the Allies had landed at Normandy and were repulsing German forces from France.

At about 300 feet, the engine suddenly died.

The morning was dry and bright, a good day for flying. Powell and the three other pilots in his formation waited for the signal. When they saw it, the four planes rolled down the grass airfield and rose into the sky.

At about 300 feet, the engine suddenly died. Powell looked out and saw flames. He also saw trees at the end of the airfield. He was flying toward them at more than one hundred miles an hour. The fire started so quickly that Powell didn't have time to feel fear. His flying instructors had told him that the best way to crash-land was to fly the plane straight. A plane can stall when turned under certain conditions, which could result in flipping it and killing the pilot.

To avoid the trees, Powell decided to take the risk. He turned *The West "by Gawd" Virginian* slightly to the right. When he felt the plane beginning to stall, he leveled it and braced for impact. It came down in a farmer's field. Soft earth temporarily smothered the flames.

The eighty-six-gallon fuel tank behind the pilot's seat might explode, so Powell disconnected his oxygen mask and radio wires and released his shoulder straps and seat belt. He tried to open the canopy, but the emergency handle stuck. He kicked out the canopy, clambered onto the right wing, and then ran. When he was twenty or thirty yards away, the fuel tank exploded.

Twenty or thirty yards away, the fuel tank exploded.

He ran through the woods and sauntered into his squadron hut.

"It was Punchy," said his intelligence officer, Captain David Lee, on the phone. "It looks like he's had it. He was going into the trees on fire."

"The hell I have!" Powell announced.

Lee spun around. "No, no. He's here. He's okay."

The two men drove back to the burning aircraft. Members of the 328th Squadron were looking for Powell's body.

"Hey, Doc," Powell said to Dr. Kenneth Lemon, the flight surgeon. "Who was it?"

"It was Punchy," the doctor replied somberly . . . before realizing he was talking to Powell. "How the hell did you get out of that thing?"

Both men laughed, and Lemon gave Powell a hug.

Powell learned later that he'd been doubly fortunate. He'd had a particularly soft landing because the owner of the field had plowed it just the day before.

★

POWELL COMPLETED EIGHTY-SEVEN FLIGHTS DURING THE WAR.

In December 1944, he left Liverpool on a Liberty ship sailing to America. As an officer, he was entitled to better accommodations on board, but he and his fellow officers gave their quarters to wounded troops, some of whom had lost legs or arms. Powell slept in the bunks on the lower decks. He arrived back home in Wilcoe, West Virginia, on Christmas Eve, 1944. Eleven days later, he married his fiancée, Betty Wiley.

★

Bob Powell stands beside his wartime memorabilia in 2011.

THE AIR FORCE ASSIGNED POWELL TO THE FLIGHT-TEST DIVISION OF Wright-Patterson Air Force Base in Dayton, Ohio. He left the Air Force in August 1945, though he remained in the reserves and returned to West Virginia University to complete his journalism degree. After graduating, he worked as a reporter at the *Roanoke Times World* in Virginia.

When the Korean War started in 1950, the Air Force recalled Powell, who was working at the Norfolk & Western Railway in Roanoke. He expected to fly P-51s in Korea, but he served as a pilot and public relations officer for an Air Force exhibit group at Wright-Patterson. After two years at the base, Powell went to the air war college at Maxwell Air

Force Base in Montgomery, Alabama, where he studied to become an instructor. When the Air Force assigned him to Grove City College in Pennsylvania, he left the Air Force for a second time and returned to the Norfolk & Western as its advertising manager.

Even after he left the Air Force, Powell maintained his interest in aviation. He helped organize the Eighth Air Force Historical Society and the 352nd Fighter Group Association. Throughout his military career, Powell had more adventures than he could have imagined as a youngster making toy airplanes and just hoping to be able to get off the ground.

THE COLOR BARRIER

ALEXANDER JEFFERSON
Second Lieutenant
301st Squadron
332nd Fighter Group
US Army Air Forces

A S A YOUNG BOY GROWING UP ON TWENTY-EIGHTH STREET IN Detroit, Alexander Jefferson dreamed of becoming a pilot. In grades three, four, and five, he often sneaked out of class at Newberry Elementary School and walked several miles to the Haggerty Field airstrip to look at the planes and talk to the pilots. Sometimes they gave him rides.

Little Alex made his own model planes, drawing the plans from photos in newspapers. He also read *Flying Aces*, a magazine filled with adventure stories about military aviators. In the early 1930s, however, the Air Corps didn't accept applications from black men. Like many other American organizations in the first half of the twentieth century, the US military was segregated, more concerned with the color of an applicant's skin than his resume. But in January 1941, the War Department announced a program to train black Americans at the Tuskegee Institute in Alabama; they would serve in segregated squadrons.

★

AFTER GRADUATING FROM HIGH SCHOOL, JEFFERSON STUDIED CHEMISTRY and biology at Clark College in Atlanta. He heard about the attack on Pearl Harbor while in a chemistry lab. He graduated in 1942 and returned to Detroit, where he applied to join the Army Air Forces (the

The War Department announced a program to train black Americans at the Tuskegee Institute.

Even in uniform, Jefferson and his comrades were judged not by their rank, skill, or courage but by their color.

---

new name for the Air Corps). He passed the written test but failed the physical because he weighed 115.5 pounds—half a pound less than the minimum requirement of 116 pounds. He gorged himself on bananas and water, retook the physical, and passed. But he had to wait until a training position opened up at the institute. In the meantime, he went to Washington, DC, and enrolled in graduate courses in the Chemistry Department at Howard University.

In April 1943, two years after he enlisted, the AAF called Jefferson to start flight training. The segregated train that he took to Tuskegee didn't offer food or provide toilets for black passengers—even those prepared to risk their lives to defend their country.

★

THE ARMY AIR FORCES DESIGNED THE TUSKEGEE TRAINING PROGRAM TO ensure that graduates could cope with the physical, mental, and emotional stress of combat missions. But even in uniform, Jefferson and his comrades were judged not by their rank, skill, or courage but by their color.

They were called up to go overseas and had to travel to Virginia to board a ship at Camp Patrick Henry. The ticket agent at the Walterboro, South Carolina, station directed them to the back window to exchange their travel vouchers for train tickets. Jefferson and his colleagues refused to obey. They insisted that she serve them at the front window, officially designated for white passengers only. The confrontation escalated, and the fifteen airmen picked up their submachine guns, which prompted the town sheriff and half a dozen white residents to rush to the station with shotguns. When the airmen upped the ante and loaded ammunition clips into their guns, officials called out the colonel of the Walterboro base to negotiate with them. He encouraged the airmen to give up their weapons, but they refused. At that point, the train engineer, in an effort to end the confrontation, told the men to get on board. Jefferson and his colleagues assumed they would be arrested at Camp Patrick Henry, but they were allowed to proceed to their barracks and to keep their firearms.

The fifteen airmen boarded a ship for Oran, Algeria, on June 3, 1944. From there they sailed to Naples, Italy. After some sightseeing, they traveled across Italy by truck to the Ramitelli Air Base, near the Adriatic Sea. There, Second Lieutenant Alexander Jefferson joined the 332nd Fighter Group's 301st Squadron as a replacement pilot. All the pilots who flew with the 332nd were black. For identification purposes, the planes of each fighter group had a different tail color. The 332nd's were painted bright red, so the group became known as "Red Tails."

Flying in a P-51 fighter, Jefferson escorted B-17 and B-24 bombers to targets ranging from France to Greece. He also participated in strafing flights against German ground targets. When the 301st gave Jefferson his own plane, he named it *Margo*, after a friend back in Washington, DC.

The town sheriff and half a dozen white residents rushed to the station with shotguns.

★

ON AUGUST 12, THE PILOTS OF THE 301ST SQUADRON FLEW TO TOULON ON the south coast of France to strafe German radar towers on a large cliff. The Allies were preparing to launch Operation Dragoon, an amphibious invasion of Marseilles, also known as the second invasion of France. Without the radar towers, the Germans wouldn't be able to locate Allied ships in the Mediterranean as the invasion started.

As Jefferson flew the *Margo* closer to the towers, his squadron leader told the four pilots to drop their external fuel tanks in order to fly faster. Jefferson's tanks stuck, though, and when they finally dropped he had to fly at maximum speed, about 425 miles an hour, to catch up to the other planes. His engine overheated; the plane shuddered. German anti-aircraft guns fired from the cliff at the P-51s, striking the plane flying three hundred feet to his right. With smoke trailing behind him, Jefferson's friend Lieutenant Bob Daniels flew out to sea. But Jefferson focused on his .50-caliber machine guns.

Seconds later, as he flew fifty feet over the towers, he heard a loud noise and felt air rush through the cockpit. The canopy had a hole in it. Flames were leaping through another hole in the floor. He had to get out.

He climbed to a higher altitude so he could bail. He pulled a red knob on his instrument panel to open the canopy and released his

The canopy had a hole in it. Flames were leaping through another hole in the floor. He had to get out.

A German soldier approached
and pointed a gun at him.

safety belt. At about 800 feet, he ejected from the *Margo*. He yanked the red D-ring to open his parachute, but nothing happened. Midair, he remembered a rumor he had heard at Ramitelli that someone was stealing the silk from parachutes to sell it. Each second felt like an eternity. *Open now,* he thought as the ground rushed toward him. The parachute blossomed open just seconds before he plunged through some trees. He landed on his feet, with only a few cuts and bruises. Then a German soldier approached and pointed a gun at him.

Some of the pilots in the 301st Squadron knew that Jefferson's plane had been hit, but they didn't see Jefferson bail out. They assumed the worst. As a result, the Tuskegee airman's parents soon received a telegram informing them that their son had died in action.

★

NAZI SOLDIERS TOOK JEFFERSON'S CIGARETTES, PEN, AND WRISTWATCH and drove him to a villa a few miles east of Toulon. They presented him to a German officer sitting on a veranda. The officer had studied political science in America and spoke excellent English. He even knew the "colored" areas in Detroit. He thanked Jefferson for the Lucky Strikes, but Jefferson offered only his name, rank, and serial number, 0819461. They transferred him to an airfield north of Toulon and held him in a barracks there for the night.

The next day, Jefferson came across Bob Daniels, the pilot whose plane was also shot down. Daniels had been afraid to bail out, so he had ditched his plane in the Mediterranean and waited for the Germans to rescue him.

Two German army guards escorted them from the South of France to the Dulag Luft interrogation center at Wetzlar, about thirty miles north of Frankfurt. They traveled by bus, train, truck, and foot, sometimes sleeping in barns. In one barn in France, they met another black prisoner, Lieutenant Richard Macon, a member of the 99th Squadron. Macon had been shot down at Montpellier, about one hundred miles west of Toulon. He was suffering from an injured neck, but the guards treated him and the other two prisoners well, sharing their food and saluting them.

At the interrogation center, Jefferson was photographed and fingerprinted. The Germans put him in a cell by himself and allowed him to shower. They also gave him the first hot meal he'd had since he'd been shot down.

After a few days, Jefferson was taken to an interrogation room. The officer, like the one at Toulon, spoke excellent English. He had a copy of a book about the Tuskegee Airmen and pointed to a photo of Jefferson on his graduation day. He also had information about Jefferson's family and a copy of an inspection report on Jefferson's plane. Someone at the Ramitelli base was supplying information to the Germans.

Someone at the Ramitelli base was supplying information to the Germans.

Accompanied by two guards, Jefferson, Daniels, and Macon went by train to Stalag Luft III. At one station, Hitler Youth in Nazi uniforms were singing a marching song. They spotted the American fliers and spewed obscenities at them. Older Germans joined them. Jefferson was terrified. The guards threatened to shoot at the mob. Only after they boarded their train did the five prisoners relax.

★

JEFFERSON ARRIVED AT STALAG LUFT III ON AUGUST 26, ONE OF THIRTEEN Tuskegee Airmen at the prison camp during the war. The Germans took him to the South Compound, designated for American prisoners of war. The compound was overcrowded, so representatives of the rooms had to select new prisoners to join them. One said his group would accept Jefferson, but the man's strong southern accent worried Jefferson, who feared the southerner wanted to humiliate him. A colonel ordered Jefferson to accept the southerner's invitation.

In Block 128, Room 8, the Tuskegee airman realized that he had nothing to fear. They were stockpiling and storing escape material, such as passports. The men wanted someone whom they could trust, someone who wouldn't divulge the room's secrets. They knew on sight that Jefferson wasn't a German spy. It was ironic, really: In a foreign prison camp, a white American who might have abused him back home trusted him more than he would another white American. Nor did the German guards discriminate against him, either. They respected him both as an officer and an American.

Some of the prisoners had been in the camp for so long that they didn't know the Army Air Forces were recruiting blacks. One newly arrived prisoner even hugged him and expressed his admiration for the Red Tail pilots. He didn't think the Nazis would have shot down his B-17 if the Red Tails had escorted it. Jefferson accepted his status as a prisoner of war and patiently waited for the war to end. He passed the time by drawing pictures of daily life and looking forward to Red Cross parcels to supplement the camp's food rations, which were so meager that the heavy black bread consisted partially of sawdust. Several weeks after learning incorrectly that their son had died, Jefferson's parents received the wonderful news from the Red Cross that he was in fact alive. They received the letters that he wrote them, although he never received their replies because the German infrastructure began crumbling in 1944.

★

ON JANUARY 27, 1945, JEFFERSON WAS WATCHING *YOU CAN'T TAKE IT WITH You*, the Kaufman and Hart play, staged by fellow prisoners. Colonel Charles Goodrich, the senior American officer, suddenly announced that the Germans wanted everyone to leave camp in thirty minutes. The men mused about the play's title as they quickly gathered food, clothes, and other valuable items.

Jefferson left the compound at 11 p.m. in an endless column of men walking westward into the night. Before long, they started discarding treasured belongings that weighed them down with each laborious step. Cherished photos and letters fell by the roadside. Many of the guards were in their sixties and seventies, and they too found the march exceptionally difficult. Some of the prisoners, feeling sorry for them, offered to help and even carried their rifles.

The men marched twenty miles until they came to some barns,

where they rested during the day. They picked up again the next evening, enduring temperatures of minus 10 and strong winds. Exhausted and hungry, they arrived in Muskau early the following morning. At the brick factory, the Nazis gave them bread, and they slept on hard concrete floors—but at least they were warm. After eight hours, they marched again so other prisoners who had left Stalag Luft III after them could enter and rest.

They trudged another fifteen miles and spent the next night in barns in a small village. To stay warm, they piled on top of one another. The next morning, they walked several more hours to Spremberg, where they boarded cattle cars for a miserable two-day trip. Cold and squalid, the cars had animal excrement on the floors. The men packed them to capacity, eighty to a car. Some of the cars contained tin cans for toilets, but none of the men had food or water.

On February 3, the train arrived at Moosburg, thirty miles northeast of the Dachau concentration camp. Jefferson and his fellow prisoners marched several more miles to Stalag VII-A, a massive prison camp in far worse condition than Stalag Luft III. It had no cooking facilities and little food, though prisoners did receive some Red Cross parcels. The barracks were so filthy that Jefferson slept outside in a tent.

The prisoners sometimes saw or heard Allied planes, and on one occasion they spotted P-51 fighters with the red tails of the 332nd Fighter Group, which were attacking the Moosburg train station. Everyone rushed from their barracks or tents to watch the Tuskegee Airmen fly overhead.

On April 29, a tank from General George Patton's Third Army arrived at the main gate. A camp officer waved a white flag, and in the

The Stars and Stripes rose above the camp.

early afternoon the Stars and Stripes rose above the camp. After the guards left, Jefferson and others went to camp headquarters to find their identification cards. Jefferson's, taken at the Dulag Luft interrogation center at Wetzlar a few days after he was shot down, shows an exhausted, unshaven young man.

Patton arrived two days later and ordered his officers to prepare meals for the liberated prisoners. They indulged in cognac and wine as well, but it wasn't all celebration. An American soldier mentioned a report of dead bodies nearby. They hopped on a jeep and made their way to the Dachau concentration camp, which the Americans had freed the day before.

Jefferson couldn't have prepared himself for what he witnessed. Even before entering, he could smell the sweet, sickening odor of burned human flesh. The crematorium was still so hot he couldn't touch it. Half-burned bodies lay in the open ovens. Thousands of corpses lay in piles on the grounds. Flies swarmed the bodies. Human hair and dental fixtures stood in heaps on tables. The walking skeletons of freed prisoners passed him like ghosts, their bodies so emaciated he didn't know how they were still alive.

The crematorium was still so hot he couldn't touch it.

"Whites to the right, niggers to the left."

Jefferson flew to France on May 9, and then to Camp Lucky Strike, near Le Havre. Camp staff there helped ready him to sail home. On May 21, he boarded the USS *Lejeune*, a troop transport ship. It docked at Southampton, England, two days later, took on additional passengers and then sailed for New York. On June 7, the Statue of Liberty came into view. Jubilation filled him. When the ship docked, Jefferson walked down the gangplank to the pier. There a white private directed the passengers: "Whites to the right, niggers to the left."

★

IN 1947, THE AIR FORCE TRIMMED ITS RANKS AND RELEASED JEFFERSON, who returned to civilian life. Initially he had trouble finding a job, despite his strong academic background. Prospective employers told him he was overqualified. An education administrator advised him that he would qualify to teach in Detroit's public schools if he earned a teaching certificate, so Jefferson went to Wayne State for a year and then joined the school system, where he taught science.

After the war, America slowly addressed the systemic discrimination that had persecuted people like Jefferson so cruelly. In 1948, President Truman signed an executive order desegregating the armed forces. The Tuskegee Airmen had shown that blacks could perform just as well as their white comrades—sometimes better. In the 1950s and '60s, the civil rights movement overturned the Jim Crow laws that had

Alexander Jefferson in 2010.

The Tuskegee Airmen had shown that blacks could perform just as well as their white comrades—sometimes better.

institutionalized segregation since the Civil War. Since then, the Tuskegee Airmen have become rightfully famous both in America and overseas.

Jefferson remained in the Air Force reserves for more than two decades and retired as a lieutenant colonel in 1969. In 1972, he helped form the Detroit chapter of the Tuskegee Airmen, and three years later he served on the board of the Tuskegee Airmen National Historical Museum. Richard Macon, one of the airmen who assisted him, had done time at Stalag Luft III with him. In 2007, President George W. Bush presented him with the Congressional Gold Medal, the highest civilian award for achievements that have made an impact on American history and culture.

As Jefferson and I spoke in the foyer of his apartment building, two young black men approached us. One asked if Jefferson was a Tuskegee Airman. Jefferson replied that he was.

"You're a celebrity!" the second man said. "They made a movie about Tuskegee Airmen."

"I did what I had to do to survive," Jefferson told me. "When I show the Tuskegee Museum to schoolchildren, I hope I show them what it means to be an American. To do the right thing and treat people right and be proud of who you are. That's what the Red Tails stood for."

MISSION TO REMEMBER

GEORGE H. W. BUSH

Lieutenant Junior Grade

Torpedo Squadron 51

US Navy

I N THE PILOTS' READY ROOM ON THE USS *SAN JACINTO*, LIEUTENANT Junior Grade George Bush joked with Lieutenant Junior Grade Ted White about bailing out of the Avenger they were about to fly. White, a gunnery officer, wanted to test the Avenger's guns in a combat situation. Bush, twenty years old, served with Squadron VT-51, based on the *San Jacinto* and consisting of nine Avenger torpedo bombers. The vessel also carried twenty-six Hellcats, fighters used to attack enemy aircraft.

Bush and other Avenger pilots had faced heavy anti-aircraft fire the previous day when they flew to Chichi Jima, a Japanese island in the Bonin Islands about six hundred miles south of Tokyo. They hadn't destroyed all the targets. They were returning to attack a radio communications center. Ordnanceman Second Class Leo Nadeau, Bush's regular turret gunner, had agreed to let White take his place. Completing the flight roster was Radioman Second Class John Delaney. The morning of September 2, 1944, began well enough, but none of the three men knew what lay in store for them that fateful day.

At 7:15 a.m., Bush revved the engine and pulled up from the *San Jacinto*, climbing to 12,000 feet for the fifty-mile trip and leaving the cockpit hatch open . . . just in case he encountered any serious danger. Three other Avengers joined them to attack the communications center, with Hellcats escorting the Avengers.

None of the three men knew what lay in store for them that fateful day.

Bush reached Chichi Jima in about an hour. The Japanese were ready. They fired anti-aircraft shells at the attacking planes. Exploding shells formed thick black clouds in the sky. Lieutenant Commander Don Melvin led the raid, dropping his bombs directly on the radio tower. Bush arrived at the island shortly after Melvin and dived toward the tower.

The lower part of Bush's fuselage sustained a hit that jolted the aircraft. Smoke spewed into the cockpit. A line of flames erupted on the wing, not far from a fuel tank. Bush was in dire trouble, but he continued to the communications tower and dropped four 500-pound bombs. Then he flew back out to sea.

Lieutenant Junior Grade Nat Adams, one of the Hellcat pilots, saw smoke coming from Bush's Avenger and heard Bush on the radio telling Delaney and White to bail out.

Turning around, Bush couldn't see White in the turret, so he assumed the gunner had left his position to prepare to bail. After sending a message to his squadron to report the hit and his plan to bail out, Bush flew the aircraft to his right to reduce the airflow on that side of the Avenger. The exit door for Delaney and White was on the right, so he hoped this maneuver would help his crewmates bail from the plane.

Bush still couldn't see what was happening in the middle or rear of the plane. He readied to leave. Leaving the cockpit hatch open now seemed prophetic. As he was climbing out, he realized that he had forgotten to remove his headset. After pausing to remove it, he tried to bail from the plane again. But his head struck the tail wing, and his parachute hit the same wing when he opened it too

He began his descent with a bleeding forehead and a torn chute.

quickly. He began his descent with a bleeding forehead and a torn chute.

★

BEFORE JOINING THE NAVY, BUSH WAS A STUDENT AT PHILLIPS ACADEMY in Andover, Massachusetts. He had been walking near the chapel when someone yelled across the campus that the Japanese had attacked Pearl Harbor. The news shocked the seventeen-year-old.

Bush so keenly wanted to enlist that he briefly considered joining the Royal Canadian Air Force, which accepted young applicants, but instead he decided to try to become an aviator with the US Navy. He enlisted in Boston on the first day that he legally could: June 12, 1942, the day he turned eighteen. By signing up then, Bush set aside the advice of Secretary of War Henry Stimson, who delivered the commencement speech for Bush's graduating class, to get a college education before enlisting. Stimson foresaw a long war and said the students could serve their country after they went to college.

Bush soon traveled to Chapel Hill, North Carolina, for Navy preflight training. He was the youngest student at the base and subsequently became the youngest aviator in the Navy at that time. Shortly after the attack on Pearl Harbor, Bush met Barbara Pierce at a Christmas dance.

She lived in Rye, New York, and they engaged to marry before Bush left on the *San Jacinto* for the Pacific.

★

THE TEAR IN HIS PARACHUTE MEANT THAT BUSH CAME DOWN QUICKLY. Dazed from hitting the tail wing, he loosened his harness to ready himself to slip out of it when he reached the water. As he floated down, his Avenger crashed into the ocean. He also spotted a life raft in the water. It was his own seatback rubber raft, but it had dropped down ahead of him because he had forgotten to attach it to his life jacket.

When he hit the water, not far from shore, Bush immediately looked for his two crewmates. He couldn't see them, but Japanese soldiers on Chichi Jima had seen two men bail from the plane.

Now in the water, Bush couldn't see the raft that he had spotted from above. Melvin, the squadron leader, saw both Bush and the raft and realized that Bush couldn't see it. Melvin pointed it out by flying down toward it. He also radioed Bush's position to help the Navy rescue team find him. Bush, who was wearing a life preserver, swam to the raft, inflated it, and climbed in.

Tired, Bush vomited after swallowing seawater. But he faced a greater problem: The choppy water was pushing his raft *toward* Chichi

The choppy water was pushing his raft *toward* Chichi Jima.

Jima. He didn't have an oar of any kind, so he used his hands as paddles to move away from the island.

The Japanese dispatched boats to find the downed aviators, but Adams, Lieutenant Doug West, and other pilots swooped down on the search boats, firing at them to keep them away.

West saw that Bush was injured and dropped a medical kit to him. Bush retrieved it and put antiseptic on his forehead. He also found dye in his life jacket and the raft, which he could spread on the water to help the search team spot him in the Pacific.

But he was missing a vital item that he desperately needed if he had to stay in the raft a long time: fresh water. His water container had broken when he parachuted from his plane.

He sat in the raft for several hours, remembering that Task Force 58, the carrier group to which the *San Jacinto* belonged, planned to leave the Chichi Jima area after the raid. If he wasn't rescued quickly, it might never happen. He also worried about his two crewmates, Delaney and White. He had been looking for them and sobbed when he thought of them.

Bush was scared.

★

NAVY PLANES CONTINUED TO CIRCLE THE DRIFTING PILOT. WEST POINTED one of his wings at the raft, marking its position for the crew of the USS *Finback*, a submarine patrolling nearby. Traveling below the surface, the *Finback* moved closer.

Bush didn't know whether the sub was American or Japanese.

Bush saw a black dot about one hundred yards away. The dot grew bigger.

It was the *Finback*'s periscope. Captain Robert Williams Jr., the submarine's commanding officer, had used it to locate the airman. Having spotted the missing pilot, Williams brought the submarine to the surface. The conning tower emerged, followed by the hull. For a moment, Bush didn't know whether the sub was American or Japanese. But as it neared, he realized it was the former.

A sailor helped him climb onto the *Finback* while the sub's photographic officer, Ensign Bill Edwards, filmed the rescue from the conning tower with a movie camera. Sailors on deck quickly brought Bush down the tower. Then the submarine slipped beneath the surface, beyond the view of Japanese soldiers.

★

THE FOLLOWING DAY, BUSH REMEMBERED BANTERING WITH WHITE ABOUT bailing out. In a letter to his parents, he reflected that he no longer thought the subject appropriate for banter. Nor was he the only Navy aviator on the *Finback*. He had joined three other previously rescued airmen. Despite telling his crewmates to leave the plane, he felt responsible for whatever had happened to them.

Bush saw the war from a different perspective.

Aboard the submarine, Bush saw the war from a different perspective. Aviators more often than not could see their foes and fire at them. Submariners, on the other hand, often didn't know the exact location of their enemies or when depth charges might explode all around them. Underwater military service frightened him more than the perils of flying.

The rescued pilots became unofficial members of the crew. When the sub surfaced, they served as lookouts on the conning tower, watching for Japanese aircraft that might attack the sub.

The four aviators stayed on the *Finback* for a month before it docked at Midway Island, where it discharged them. Bush then flew to Pearl Harbor. At that point, he was entitled to return home on leave, but instead he returned to the *San Jacinto*, rejoining his squadron at Ulithi in the Caroline Islands eight weeks after his bombing raid on Chichi Jima. The carrier sailed toward the Philippines.

Sailors from the USS *Finback* help George H. W. Bush aboard after he was shot down over the Pacific.

In December 1944, another squadron replaced VT-51 on the *San Jacinto*, and Bush returned to America.

On Christmas Eve, he arrived at Rye, where Barbara, his fiancée, lived. Two weeks later they married.

★

THE NAVY REASSIGNED BUSH TO SQUADRON VT-153. HE EXPECTED TO return to the Pacific later in the war to participate in the invasion of Japan, which he feared would prove exceptionally bloody. But President Truman's decision to drop atomic bombs on Hiroshima and Nagasaki brought the war to an end.

Bush was based at the Oceana Naval Air Station at Virginia Beach, Virginia, on August 14, 1945, when Japan surrendered. The whole city celebrated by marching into the streets, bringing with them joy, relief, and plenty of liquid refreshments. After celebrating, the Bushes went to church to remember those who had died and to express their appreciation that the war had ended.

In all, Bush flew fifty-eight combat missions and received the Distinguished Flying Cross for heroism and extraordinary achievement during his flight to Chichi Jima. The Navy discharged him in September 1945, and he enrolled at Yale University, where he studied economics.

In April 1946, eight months after the war with Japan had ended, Bush learned that two Japanese officers had been charged with war crimes for executing American aviators shot down over the Bonin Islands and for practicing cannibalism.

After graduating, Bush moved to Texas, where he entered the oil business and later the political arena.

★

One of the first decisions that President Bush had to make was whether to attend the emperor's state funeral.

WHEN BUSH RAN FOR VICE PRESIDENT ON THE REPUBLICAN TICKET IN 1980, Bill Edwards, the photographic officer on the *Finback*, contacted him to say he had the film of his rescue.

After serving as President Reagan's vice president for eight years, Bush became the forty-first president of the United States. Two weeks before he took the Oath of Office, however, Emperor Hirohito of Japan—the man who stood at the apex of the imperial Japanese war effort—died. One of the first decisions that President Bush had to make was whether to attend the emperor's state funeral the next month. Bush chose to go. Over more than four decades, Japan had become a friend and ally to America, and the positive changes that occurred in postwar Japan offered a valuable lesson.

Bush emphasized this point when he spoke on December 7, 1991, at a ceremony commemorating the fiftieth anniversary of the attack on Pearl Harbor. He told veterans and their families that he felt no rancor toward Japan or Germany.

In 2002, Bush returned to Chichi Jima—in circumstances very different from those of September 2, 1944. Japan's military helped him find the spot where he had been shot down. Bush placed wreaths in the water at that location to honor the two men he never forgot: Radioman Second Class John Delaney and Lieutenant Junior Grade Ted White.

Bush's harrowing experiences during World War II stayed with him long after the war ended. They gave him an appreciation for teamwork and a feeling of pride. He also never forgot that his comrades went out of their way to save a scared young airman floating in a raft on the vast ocean.

★　★　★

President Bush parachutes onto the campus of the George Bush Presidential Library and Museum at College Station, Texas, during the library's tenth anniversary ceremony in 2007.

THE MYSTERIOUS PILOT

BRUCE MARTIN
Second Lieutenant
352nd Squadron
301st Bomb Group
US Army Air Forces

B RUCE MARTIN WAS WORKING FOR AIRCRAFT MANUFACTURER Curtiss-Wright in Buffalo, New York, when news broke about the attack on Pearl Harbor. The next day, a guard on the roof of the plant was brandishing a machine gun.

The war is here, he thought.

He was drafted into the US Army, but he wanted to fly a B-17 bomber, so he applied to serve in the Army Air Forces and was accepted.

★

SECOND LIEUTENANT BRUCE MARTIN WAS FLYING HIS B-17—KNOWN BY ITS number, 499—to take out an oil refinery at Blechhammer in eastern Germany on October 14, 1944. The 499 was one of five bombers from the 352nd Squadron of the 301st Bomb Group, based at Foggia, in southern Italy, en route to German targets. But the flight engineer, Staff Sergeant Paul Shultz, had some disturbing news: "We consumed more fuel than we should have by this time. We're going to be short."

Martin had grown up on a farm near Medina in upstate New York, so he knew how to deal with unforeseen mechanical problems. The twenty-six-year-old kept the B-17 in formation and, to reduce their load, released two 500-pound bombs over a wheat field. When they reached their target, they dropped the remaining six bombs.

Even with a lighter payload, though, they probably didn't have enough fuel to make it all the way back to Foggia. The Royal Air Force

"We're going to be short."

"Hold your fire," Martin ordered.

maintained a base in the Adriatic Sea on the Isle of Vis, controlled by the Yugoslav Resistance. That they could make.

He radioed the lead plane in his formation and told the pilot, Second Lieutenant Bill Barkman, what he wanted to do. Barkman advised that Martin should stay in formation; a German fighter might attack a bomber flying on its own. But if Martin tried to make it all the way back to Foggia and ran out of fuel, he'd have to ditch 499 in the Adriatic.

About halfway between Blechhammer and Vis, one of the crew inter-commed Martin to ask if they should jettison items to reduce the aircraft's weight. No, he wasn't so desperate that he wanted to lose the bomber's equipment. Later, another crewman asked if they should prepare to bail.

"No," Martin replied. "Only as a last resort." The crew would be safer in the aircraft than bailing out over Austria. "Try to relax," he added. "Keep watch for fighters."

About two hours into their return flight, Sergeant Gerald O. Shasteen, the tail gunner, spotted another aircraft half a mile away.

"There's a fighter plane coming up on us," Shasteen said, but he couldn't identify it.

"Hold your fire," Martin ordered.

A few minutes passed. The gunners on 499 held their fingers nervously on their triggers, ready to fire. The mysterious aircraft approached 499 on its right side.

"It looks like a P-38," Shasteen said. The P-38 was an American fighter, easily identifiable by its two fuselages.

"Hold your fire," Martin repeated.

A voice came over the bomber's radio. It was the P-38 pilot: "Are you going to make it?" he asked. He must have heard Martin's conversation with Barkman about flying to Vis.

"We're going to try," Martin said.

The P-38 flew in tight formation beside the B-17. Martin looked into the cockpit of the P-38 and noticed that the pilot was black. He didn't know the Army Air Forces had accepted black pilots, but he also didn't care. He was grateful that the flier was escorting him while he was short of fuel.

"I'm going to have to leave," the P-38 pilot announced after about fifteen minutes. He, too, was probably low on fuel.

Martin's fuel tanks were nearing empty, but he still had half an hour to go to reach Vis.

Within a couple of minutes of landing, he contacted the tower at the air base. "I'm 499 on my approach," he said. "Request landing instructions."

"Four-nine-nine, go around," a controller replied.

He wasn't sure he had enough fuel to bring 499 down—let alone fly around the air base. No one was going to tell him not to land. Martin threw his headset on the floor.

"Did you hear what the tower said?" Second Lieutenant Robert E. Lee, the copilot, asked.

"Screw the tower!" Martin replied. "We're going down."

The instrument panel showed that the inner right engine had run out of fuel. Seconds later, Martin landed the bomber smoothly on the

"Screw the tower! We're going down."

"You can put me before a firing squad, but I'm not going to fly that plane again."

grass runway. As soon as they stopped, a member of the Royal Air Force ran out to the bomber and told the crew to get out and run. The 499 was blocking the runway, and another plane might crash into theirs.

The crew ran, but a few of them stopped to kiss the ground, thankful to have landed safely. After moving the B-17, which normally held about two thousand gallons of fuel, they discovered it had only seven gallons left.

★

MARTIN AND HIS CREW STAYED OVERNIGHT ON VIS AND FLEW BACK TO Foggia the next morning with a full tank. The next day, October 16, 1944, they made another bombing run to Blechhammer. Once again, 499 didn't have enough fuel for the return flight to Foggia. Once again, Martin had to land and refuel on Vis.

Back in Italy, he reported his concerns to Lieutenant Colonel Leslie Holman, a senior officer with 301st Bomb Group.

"You can put me before a firing squad, but I'm not going to fly that plane again," Martin said.

Holman asked mechanics to check the aircraft. The plane was burning too much fuel because a previous ground crew hadn't adjusted its carburetion system for combat flying.

★

MARTIN COMPLETED HIS TOUR AND RETURNED TO THE STATES IN December 1944, sailing from Naples to New York in a Liberty ship. He remained with the Army Air Forces until the war ended, serving in a training role.

After the war, he worked in a chemical factory in Middleport, New York. In 1953 he took up the family business, farming. He bought a farm near Medina and grew tomatoes and cabbages.

Over the years, he wondered about the P-38 pilot, particularly after President George W. Bush awarded the Congressional Gold Medal to the Tuskegee Airmen in 2007. Military records show that on October 14, 1944, the Tuskegee Airmen based in Italy flew P-51s. Nor did the P-38 have a red tail. But Martin never forgot the pilot who flew by his side, ready to help during a long and difficult flight.

Bruce Martin died in 2011 at the age of ninety-three. The identity of the other pilot remains a mystery.

Bruce Martin on his farm in 2010.

IGNITION TROUBLE

CASS PHILLIPS
Lieutenant
Patrol Bombing Squadron 20
US Navy

S HORTLY BEFORE 8 A.M. ON DECEMBER 7, 1941, CASS PHILLIPS WAS on his way to get breakfast at the Kaneohe Naval Air Station on the east coast of Oahu when he saw a low-flying plane bearing a sun on its wings and fuselage. The Army Air Forces had been conducting exercises in the area, so he assumed it was an American plane, figuring they were making it realistic by putting authentic Japanese insignia on the plane.

When he arrived at the station's restaurant, Phillips noticed two women who worked there. Frightened, they were looking out a window at planes on fire about two hundred yards away. Phillips looked for himself and saw bombs falling on hangars and PBY Catalina seaplanes.

Phillips—a twenty-one-year-old radioman from Riverside, California, who was flying with the Navy—immediately ran to the hangars to help extinguish the fires and help the wounded. A sailor with a stomach injury called for someone to move his legs. Phillips tried but couldn't make the sailor comfortable. Smoke billowed into the sky. All the planes in the area except two lay in flames or on their sides.

Some of the men tried to pull the .50-caliber machine guns from the planes to fire at the Japanese aircraft, but no one expected further fire from above.

"Here they come again!" a sailor yelled.

Japanese planes roared overhead and strafed the base. Seeking shelter, Phillips ran to a large hole dug in the ground for fuel tanks.

"Here they come again!" a sailor yelled.

When he realized that it wasn't going to offer adequate protection, he went into a hangar that he believed had concrete walls. But they were made of asbestos rather than concrete. A bomb fell on the hangar, and they collapsed. Phillips wasn't hurt, but eighteen sailors at Kaneohe died during the attack.

The attack proved so successful that almost everyone at the station thought the Japanese were going to invade Hawaii. The men on base didn't have camouflage clothing, so within hours the Navy stuffed their white uniforms into a large vat of boiling tea to stain them dark beige. Then the men donned their still-wet tea-stained uniforms.

The tense sailors succumbed to fear. One raced into a barracks to tell everyone to run for high ground. "I sniffed the mist, and it's gas!" he said.

It was just fog.

★

A FEW WEEKS AFTER THE ATTACK, PHILLIPS WAS ACCEPTED AS A STUDENT at a Navy flight school in Pensacola, Florida. Six months later, Lieutenant Phillips became a PBY pilot. At first, he flew with the VP-61 squadron at Alameda, California, and then from the Aleutian Islands off the coast of Alaska.

He later joined a new squadron, VPB-20, in the western Pacific to fly PBMs—bigger, faster seaplanes than he had flown previously. During late 1944, the squadron went to Manus, an island off the north coast of New Guinea, to prepare to move closer to Japan. On January 9, 1945, the squadron moved to the Lingayen Gulf off the island of Luzon to support the campaign to remove Japanese forces from the Philippines. In the afternoon, Phillips flew to the eastern side of the gulf and refueled at the tender ship the USS *Currituck*. The crew dropped anchor about a quarter mile from shore. Several other PBMs were also in the gulf.

Men were walking near a small building onshore, but Phillips wasn't worried. They'd had no intel that hostile troops were in the area. He rested up in a bunk to prepare for a long night patrol. Some of his fellow crewmembers went out on a wing to relax and enjoy the warm weather. That's when they heard mortar shells and machine-gun bullets. They ran into the fuselage as quickly as they could, shouting that the plane was under attack.

Phillips bolted upright. He hadn't expected Japanese forces to be nearby. He hurried to the cockpit. Ensign Jim Wall, the copilot, arrived first and pulled an ignition knob to start the two engines. Phillips entered the cockpit right after him but didn't realize that Wall had pulled the knob already. In the confusion, Phillips put his hand on the knob and pushed it, switching off the ignition.

While the two men were trying to start the plane, mortar shells hit the water. Two shells landed behind the plane, then two in front. They feared the next set of shells would prove more accurate. Machine-gun bullets sprayed the water fifty to a hundred feet from the plane.

"What the hell's going on up there?"

Phillips's mouth went bitter and dry. He pulled the ignition knob. The engines still didn't start. He called Jack Waterman, the mechanic, on the intercom. "What the hell's going on up there?"

Waterman checked his gauges. "I'm not sure, but everything looks fine here."

Phillips looked again at the instrument panel and realized that neither he nor the copilot had turned on the master switch. He flipped the switch, and the engines started immediately.

But even with the engines operating, Phillips couldn't move the plane away from the mortar shells and machine-gun bullets fast enough. The crew had to bring up the anchor slowly to avoid damaging the plane. Rod Sellars, the radioman, carefully turned the anchor crank. After a long minute—in which they miraculously sustained no mortar or machine-gun fire—the anchor came to the surface. Phillips moved the plane away from shore, away from the bullets and shells, away from danger.

He revved the engines to where they could rise above the eight- to ten-foot waves that were rocking the plane. Then he and his crew flew off to spend a long night patrolling the Philippine Islands, as did the other seaplanes in the gulf.

By the time they returned the next morning, American troops once again had made the area safe for the seaplanes.

★

PHILLIPS SERVED IN THE PACIFIC THEATER UNTIL HE RETURNED TO THE United States shortly before the war ended. He remained in the

Navy, retiring as a lieutenant commander in 1960 and moving to Pensacola.

His simple advice about what he learned from his ordeal on January 9, 1945: "Try to keep your head and be able to check through the procedures to find where it went wrong."

In 2012, Cass Phillips notes on an atlas some of the Pacific Islands he saw during the war.

DEVOUT DUTY

HERMAN ECHSNER
Sergeant
746th Squadron
456th Bomb Group
US Army Air Forces

E ARLY IN THE MORNING OF DECEMBER 8, 1941, HERMAN ECHSNER went to the depot of the *Louisville Courier-Journal* to pick up the newspapers for delivery.

"You're going to have plenty of news this morning," the man in charge told Echsner. The front-page headline screamed what Echsner and millions of other Americans would be talking about: "Japs Bomb Hawaii, Guam."

As a devout Catholic, Echsner felt a duty to join the armed forces immediately. But he was only sixteen years old, a student at St. Xavier High School in Louisville, Kentucky. When the time came, he went to St. Louis to take the Navy's aviation test. He couldn't finish the test in the time allotted, but he didn't give up. He took the Army Air Forces test in Louisville and passed, proudly joining the cadet program on July 4, 1943.

★

AFTER FINISHING HIS TRAINING PROGRAM TO BECOME A TAIL GUNNER OF a B-24 Liberator, Sergeant Herman Echsner joined the crew of First Lieutenant Joe Raker, who had flown a crop duster in Kansas before the war. Raker's crew was based at Cerignola, in south-central Italy, with the 746th Squadron of the 456th Bomb Group.

On February 16, 1945, Echsner's eighth mission was to attack

"You're going to have plenty of news this morning."

Echsner silently recited an act
of contrition for his sins.

a strategic air base at Regensburg in southeast Germany, where Messerschmitt jets were made. A briefing officer warned them that they might fly into heavy anti-aircraft fire. Also, the Allies were cutting German fuel supplies, but they might come face-to-face with German fighters.

Early in the morning, the crew took off in *Gravel Gertie*, named for a character in the *Dick Tracy* comic strip. At 23,000 feet, the temperature outside the aircraft was minus 30 degrees, but the sky gave them a clear view of the majestic Alps.

As the squadron approached the air base, the Germans fired anti-aircraft shells. Red flashes and heavy smoke slashed and blackened the air. An exploding shell created a whomping noise that sounded like a bat hitting a washtub. Echsner silently recited an act of contrition for his sins. Raker, the pilot, watched the lead plane to know when to order his crew to drop their 100-pound fragmentation bombs. Fortunately for the whole crew, no German fighters targeted them.

Flak struck *Gravel Gertie* near the air base. Raker turned her around to head back to Cerignola, but two engines, one on each side, had failed. He feathered their propellers, turning the blades inward to prevent them from slowing the aircraft.

They had to leave the formation and fly home alone. Raker wasn't sure they could make it. To save fuel, he instructed everyone to toss any heavy objects, such as guns and ammunition, from the waist gunners'

Minute by minute, mile by mile, the plane lost altitude.

windows. He set a course along the Adriatic coast so that they could make an emergency landing on water or land. Echsner would have preferred to stay in the tail turret looking after the rear guns, but he helped the others throw out heavy items. Minute by minute, mile by mile, the plane lost altitude.

"We don't have enough fuel to get home," Raker announced, "but we don't know where we are. We're going down. Vote: beach or water." One by one, the crew voted unanimously for a beach landing.

As they flew along the coast, the crew saw the wreckage of two planes on the beach. When they were flying only a few hundred feet above ground, a P-38 fighter appeared beside them. Flak had damaged the radio, so the crew couldn't communicate with the pilot. They gave him the thumbs-down sign to show that they were in distress and might crash-land and to let the base know. Raker remained silent as he brought the plane down. The wheels lowered, and the crew braced themselves. Echsner sat on the floor with his back against a wall.

The sand slowed the aircraft, which slid into it as it skidded to a halt.

The wheels lowered, and the crew braced themselves.

Everyone hid behind a sand dune and pulled out their .45s.

Several fliers were hurt, but all walked out of the plane. Echsner suffered only an injured finger.

Had they flown south enough to reach the Allied-controlled part of Italy, or were they still in the northern section controlled by the Nazis? They were about to find out. About half a mile away, a truck was speeding toward them. They couldn't tell whether it was American or German, so everyone hid behind a sand dune and pulled out their .45s. When the truck was within a hundred yards, they could see it was American.

They holstered their guns and emerged from behind the dune. The truck driver wore an American Army uniform with three stripes. He was a sergeant. He'd seen the plane coming down and came out to look for them. They had landed in Termoli, near the line dividing the Allies and the Germans, who were only four miles away. He took them into town, where they enjoyed pasta and wine with a local family.

That night, in an infantry tent, Echsner and his crewmates heard guns firing at the front. The next day the sergeant drove them to Cerignola. Echsner never learned whether the P-38 pilot had alerted the base about their condition, but the 456th Bomb Group abandoned *Gravel Gertie* on the beach.

★

German anti-aircraft guns fell silent.

ECHSNER COMPLETED HIS TOUR ON APRIL 25, 1945. HIS TWENTY-FIFTH mission was a bombing raid on Linz, Austria, in *Heavenly Body*, a B-24. The anti-aircraft fire was heavy that day, too, and shrapnel struck the plane. One piece hit Echsner's helmet but didn't injure him.

Entitled to R&R, the crew headed for Capri on May 8. On the ferry, they learned that Germany had surrendered. The war in Europe had ended. German anti-aircraft guns fell silent. Raker and his crew flew over several cities in Austria that they had targeted. The cities were clearing the bombed areas with impressive speed.

The *Heavenly Body* crew left Cerignola to start the long trip back to America. They stopped in Dakar in French West Africa (now Senegal)

for a brief but well-deserved holiday engineered when Raker falsely reported that the plane had developed engine trouble.

After the war, Echsner practiced medicine in Columbus, Indiana. Looking back on his twenty-five missions, he was aware every time he flew that he might die, but he knew he would have another life. What mattered to him was that his conscience was clear and he had done his best.

In 2012, Herman Echsner flips through the pages of a book that he wrote about his life.

★ ★ ★

MISS STEVE

BILL CULLERTON
Lieutenant
357th Fighter Squadron
355th Fighter Group
US Army Air Forces

ON APRIL 8, 1945, LIEUTENANT BILL CULLERTON AND FIFTEEN other fighter pilots were escorting B-24 bombers flying to Germany, ready to shoot down any German planes that approached. Based at Steeple Morden in England, Cullerton flew a P-51 Mustang, a small single-seater that he had named *Miss Steve* after his fiancée, Elaine Stephen.

After the fighter pilots successfully escorted the bombers, they looked for a target to attack. In the early afternoon, Cullerton, the squadron leader, spotted an airfield at Ansbach, about twenty-five miles southwest of Nuremberg. Flying just ten to twenty feet above the runway, he strafed the planes parked on the tarmac, turned around, and fired again, destroying several aircraft.

But then he felt a massive jolt. A shell had hit his aircraft, and the first thought that raced through his head was that he might never see Elaine again. He jerked the Mustang upward. In his rearview mirror, he could see flames shooting from the fuel tank. He pulled the red handle on the right side of the cockpit to release the canopy. *Miss Steve*, which

Bill Cullerton sits on the wing of his P-51 Mustang, *Miss Steve*, in 1944.

had been flying at about 300 miles an hour, stalled as Cullerton ejected from the cockpit.

BACK IN CHICAGO, ELAINE WAS PLANNING THEIR SUMMER WEDDING. THE previous December, home on leave after completing his first tour, Bill had proposed to her. He already had volunteered to return to Europe for a second tour. Many fighter pilots never returned home, but Elaine had no reservations. She said yes.

LIEUTENANT ROBERT GARLICH, ANOTHER PILOT IN THE 357TH SQUADRON, saw Cullerton's plane crash in flames, but he saw no parachute. Through German ground fire that hit his plane, Garlich flew back to Steeple Morden, where he told squadron officials what he saw.

Other pilots in the squadron, however, reported that they had seen a parachute, so Cullerton was listed as missing in action. Still, everyone feared that the Wisconsin native had become another casualty in the air war against Nazi Germany. He had been a superb pilot, destroying or damaging twenty-two enemy aircraft.

AS CULLERTON PULLED THE RIPCORD OF HIS PARACHUTE, HIS LUCKY Strike cigarettes, which had been in his jacket pocket, were floating in front of him. He tried to grab them, but they dropped away. The parachute

They were so close he could have touched them.

opened with a jolt. Because he had been flying so close to the ground when he bailed, he didn't have time to roll when he landed. He placed his hands behind his back to break his fall. He came down in a plowed field at the edge of the airfield. *Miss Steve* crashed and burst into flames.

Cullerton took off his chute and stashed it under a pine tree before running a hundred yards to the other side of the field, where he wrapped himself around the base of a tree trunk to blend into his surroundings. Two German soldiers walked up to the tree for a smoke break. They were so close he could have touched them. He remained frozen still, barely breathing. After several agonizing minutes, the two men walked away.

Cullerton remained under the tree until the sun set. Under cover of darkness, he got up and took stock of his survival kit: matches, chocolate bar, .45 handgun. A button on his flight suit contained a compass that he followed west, hoping to encounter American or other Allied soldiers gradually advancing into Germany. He used a couple of matches to check his direction and found that he had walked east. Then he realized that he had wasted the matches: The compass dial was phosphorescent. He was making foolish, possibly deadly mistakes.

When the sun rose on April 9, he hid among the trees again. Area farmers planted potatoes, which, after sundown, Cullerton tried to dig up. The hard ground rebuffed him, though, and he came up empty-handed. Following a trail, he came to a farmhouse, which he carefully searched for anything to eat, even garbage. Nothing.

He continued walking until he saw lights, which he feared were German troops searching for him. But a closer look revealed rotting wood emitting phosphorescent light, a phenomenon he had learned about as a fishing guide back in high school.

The next night he stumbled across a sleeping deer. It leapt up in fear and brushed against him as it ran away. But the deer had startled Cullerton as much as he had startled it. He bolted as well, running into twigs and branches in the dark. When he stopped to rest, he remembered his chocolate bar. It was the first food he had eaten since he was shot down.

Later that night he came across a stream. He jumped across it—but in the darkness he had misjudged the distance. He landed squarely in the freezing water. Now he had to wait until the morning for the sun to dry his clothes. When the sun finally lit the sky, he came across a village bridge guarded by two German soldiers. The men were too busy chatting with a couple of teenage girls to be surveying the bridge closely, but Cullerton still had to find a way across without speaking to them. He spotted a bicycle beside a building and pedaled it boldly past them. When he had reached the other side, one of the soldiers called out. He didn't know what the man was saying, so he simply replied: "Yah! Yah!"

The soldiers laughed.

Cullerton cycled for several miles and left the bike at the side of the road. He went back into the woods and found another trail. That night, in the distance, a dog was barking. But then it came closer and closer. Cullerton unholstered his handgun, braced himself on his knees, and waited. Its paws hit the ground heavily. A few yards away, as the dog lunged for him, Cullerton fired a single shot, killing the dog instantly.

One problem solved, but German soldiers might have had heard the

Cullerton unholstered his handgun, braced himself on his knees, and waited.

shot. If they did, now they knew where to look. Cullerton scrammed as quickly as he could.

The next morning, he found himself in a wooded area close to a field in which an armed German soldier was supervising farmworkers planting potatoes. A woman in her thirties wearing a babushka head scarf—probably a Russian or Polish slave laborer—was working not far away.

When the soldier had walked a quarter of a mile away, Cullerton approached her.

"Amerikanski?" she asked.

"Yes, American," he said and pointed to his stomach.

She understood and brought bread, water, and raw potatoes. The bread had maggots, which he started to remove—but eating maggots isn't hard when you're starving.

He signaled that he had to leave. She pointed to herself, indicating that she wanted to join him. Cullerton shook his head. She was safer where she was. She cried, but the Germans might find him, and they would treat her severely if they found her with him.

He continued west. After an hour, he heard artillery shells and small-arms fire in the distance. That meant he was nearing Allied soldiers. The shelling gradually grew louder as he walked. The Allies were firing "tree bursts," powerful shells in clusters of five or six, designed to explode when they hit trees, killing German soldiers hiding in the woods.

The Waffen-SS group leader came back, pointed the handgun at Cullerton's abdomen, and fired.

The Allied artillery barrage might kill him. He needed to get out of the woods. He ran up a hill, and when he looked back down a dozen German soldiers were staring at him. They wore black uniforms with lightning insignia on their collars. Cullerton didn't recognize the symbol, but they were Waffen-SS, the armed wing of the Schutzstaffel. He had no choice but to surrender.

The group leader approached, took Cullerton's .45, and returned to his men. Then he came back, pointed the handgun at Cullerton's abdomen, and fired. Cullerton fell down and lost consciousness. The Nazis left him to die.

★

IN THE DAYS THAT CULLERTON WAS TREKKING THROUGH THE WOODS, the staff at the Steeple Morden air base were deciding which of his personal belongings to send to his parents. They assembled his best uniform and a photo of Elaine. Father George McHugh, a chaplain with the 355th Fighter Group, had known the young pilot quite well. He had arranged for Cullerton's baptism into the Catholic faith and had given him a gold cross and chain that Cullerton wore around his neck.

"We spent much time together," Father McHugh wrote to Cullerton's parents, indicating that they shouldn't expect to see their son alive again.

★

THE BULLET HAD PIERCED CULLERTON'S LIVER. THE LIVER CONTAINS A large supply of blood, so a wound to it doesn't clot easily, often meaning a slow, painful death.

Cullerton regained consciousness in bright sunlight and great pain. Blood had soaked the right side of his abdomen and his back where the bullet had exited. *I'm going to bleed to death*, he thought. He lost consciousness again. When he woke, both wounds had dried. The cold April air had formed ice crystals on his eyelids and probably helped his wounds to clot.

Semiconscious, he felt a man removing his watch from his wrist. Cullerton groaned. Startled, the man pulled back, then lifted Cullerton onto a horse-drawn cart. Cullerton moaned and lost consciousness again.

★

"CAT-O-LEEK?" ASKED A MAN STANDING BESIDE CULLERTON'S GURNEY. "Cat-o-leek?"

The man had seen Cullerton's gold cross and chain and wanted to know whether he was Catholic.

"Yes," Cullerton replied hazily. "Where am I?"

He was in a hospital in Feuchtwangen, Germany. The doctor beside him indicated that he had been shot through the liver.

Newspapers covered the limbs of some of the soldiers.

"There are no priests," he said before leaning over the gurney and whispering, "I am a Jew. I will help you. My name is Meier."

Dr. Meier told Cullerton that he likely was going to bleed to death. There was nothing he could do. He offered to write a note to Cullerton's parents, but Cullerton declined. He didn't know whether he could trust the doctor.

Dr. Meier placed Cullerton in a ward with German soldiers who had been wounded while fighting the Soviets on the Eastern Front. The hospital had run out of bandages, so newspapers covered the limbs of some of the soldiers, who insisted that Dr. Meier remove the American. Cullerton got his own room, outside of which a German soldier stood guard—as much to keep the wounded Germans from attacking Cullerton as to make sure that Cullerton didn't escape.

The doctor arranged for a Dutch boy and Lutheran deaconesses to take care of Cullerton. The deaconesses brought him food and read to him from a German Bible. But the Nazis in charge of the hospital still

A German soldier stood guard—as much to keep the wounded Germans from attacking Cullerton as to make sure that Cullerton didn't escape.

wanted the American gone. Dr. Meier warned that moving Cullerton could kill him. If they ejected him, someone had to sign a form accepting responsibility for Cullerton's fate. American forces were close by, so no one wanted to take the blame. Instead, two of them came to Cullerton's room one day, dragged him down the hallway, and threw him down a flight of stairs, reopening his wounds. Furious, Dr. Meier and the Dutch boy carried Cullerton back to bed.

★

A FEW DAYS LATER, DR. MEIER REPORTED THAT NAZI TROOPS WERE retreating from the area and coming the next day to take Cullerton with them as a bargaining chip. But the doctor had prepared an escape plan for his American ward. He placed a cart filled with manure under the window of Cullerton's first-floor room. That would give the pilot a soft landing for his escape.

The Dutch boy brought Cullerton's flight suit and his personal items, including his ID card, which had a hole in it. The bullet had pierced the card, which Cullerton had kept in his front pocket. That evening, he donned his flight suit and jumped onto the manure. His wounds started bleeding, and he was in pain, but he walked for a quarter of a mile until he came across a culvert under a road. He crawled into it and fell asleep. The next morning, German tanks, trucks, and motorcycles were moving eastward above him. He fell asleep again.

"Who does Ted Williams play for?"

"This guy's drunk," he reproached the men.

More tanks rumbled in the distance the following morning—probably Americans pursuing the Germans. The noise grew louder. Cullerton peeked out and saw a long line of American tanks with white stars. He staggered toward them.

A black gunner with a submachine gun spotted Cullerton, who, holding his hands high, identified himself as an American pilot.

"Don't move," the gunner said.

With rifles at the ready, several infantrymen came down the embankment toward him.

"Who does Ted Williams play for?" one asked.

"The Boston Red Sox," Cullerton replied.

The infantrymen cheered.

They offered him brandy and boiled eggs while they waited for an ambulance. He enjoyed both—then vomited them back up.

The ambulance collected Cullerton to take him to a field hospital, but the medic noticed something unusual.

"This guy's drunk," he reproached the men.

But Cullerton was in reasonably good condition. The Waffen-SS officer had fired from only a foot away, so the bullet passed clean through Cullerton's liver. A bullet fired from a distance would have tumbled or wobbled, causing much more internal damage. Cullerton flew to an American hospital in Paris, where a doctor concluded that his wounds were healing well.

While recuperating, the pilot telegrammed his parents to let them know he was "slightly injured." Because transatlantic mail traveled slowly during the war, Orville and Ethyl Cullerton hadn't received the note from Father McHugh. They didn't know their son was missing, let alone wounded.

Cullerton wanted to return to Steeple Morden, but the hospital wanted to keep him for thirty days to recuperate. The American intelligence office on Rue La Fayette also wanted him to answer questions. The officers wanted to confirm that he hadn't shot himself—which of course he hadn't, but he had a hard time convincing them. Through an intelligence officer who was going to England, Cullerton sent a message to Father McHugh that the Americans were holding him as a "prisoner."

Within days, a hospital supervisor informed Cullerton that the Army Air Forces wanted him at Orly airfield within an hour.

"Who do you know?" the supervisor asked, surprised at the quick departure.

At Orly, the personal aircraft of Lieutenant-General James Doolittle, commander of the Eighth Air Force, was waiting to fly Cullerton back to England. Cullerton was the only passenger on the general's plane—and stunned. Had Father McHugh somehow contacted Doolittle directly? Perhaps the general was expressing his appreciation to the 355th Fighter Group for escorting him and other senior leaders on combat flights.

Back in England, Cullerton was admitted to the Wimpole Park Hospital, near Steeple Morden. Dr. Earl Walker, the fighter group's physician, declared that Cullerton was making good progress. Father McHugh visited the pilot there and confirmed that he had helped arrange the flight to England. At Wimpole Park, Cullerton also learned that Elaine had set their wedding date for June 30.

On V-E Day, May 8, 1945, Cullerton was still in the hospital, but not long afterward he flew to New York and took a train to Washington, where he underwent further interrogation.

Bill Cullerton enjoying a drive in his Mustang convertible, *Miss Steve*.

Orville and Ethyl Cullerton and Elaine Stephen joyously greeted him when he arrived at Union Station in Chicago on June 12. The reunited couple married eighteen days later, and Cullerton's father sent surgical instruments to Dr. Meier to thank him for what he had done.

Cullerton made a career in the recreational fishing business. From time to time, his doctor removed pieces of copper from the bullet that had worked its way through his body. Cullerton also suffered back problems, likely caused by his hard parachute landing.

"Don't give up," Cullerton said of his military experiences, which had taught him to watch for the unexpected and to persevere. "Don't ever give up."

Bill Cullerton died in 2013 at the age of eighty-nine. In his last years, he didn't fly P-51 Mustangs, but he did drive a 2004 Mustang convertible with a familiar name painted on its side: *Miss Steve*.

★ ★ ★

FIGHTING THE WEATHER

GEORGE MYFELT

Corporal

490th Bomb Squadron

2nd Bombardment Group

5th Combat Wing

Fifteenth Air Force

US Army Air Forces

G EORGE MYFELT, EIGHTEEN YEARS OLD, REPORTED FOR ACTIVE duty at Keesler Army Airfield in Biloxi, Mississippi, in February 1944.

More than a year later, Corporal Myfelt, a cryptographic technician, was sitting in a C-46 transport plane on an airstrip at Warazup, Burma, fearing they were going to have a difficult flight. The plane was taking members of the 490th Bomb Squadron and some of the squadron's equipment and supplies over the Himalayas to a new base in Hanchung, in central China. Storms near the Roof of the World could prove as deadly as Japanese bullets.

Despite his concerns, he was glad to be leaving Burma. The heat and humidity overwhelmed him, and the weather at Hanchung would feel more like home in Mansfield, Pennsylvania. To reach the base, the flight had three legs: Warazup to Kunming; Kunming to Chungking, provisional capital of the Republic of China; and Chungking to Hanchung.

The B-25 Mitchell bombers of the 490th Squadron had destroyed bridges used by Japanese, but the squadron was moving because the Allies had halted Japan's westward advance into India. Imperial forces had retreated to the eastern side of the Himalayas.

The C-46 took off in good weather shortly after 6 p.m., rising above the stifling heat and humidity of Burma. But after forty-five minutes the pilot saw a storm ahead of them.

Storms near the Roof of the World could prove as deadly as Japanese bullets.

"Hey, boys, it's going to be rough."

"Hey, boys, it's going to be rough," he radioed to the passengers, who were sitting on benches along the fuselage. "Better tighten up the chutes."

Lightning flashed, but the engines drowned out the noise of thunder clapping around the plane. Myfelt put on his parachute, which felt big and loose. He didn't mind flying through bad weather—he had done that before—but bailing with a loose chute didn't always end well. The pilot hoped to fly through the storm, but all he could see were rain and lightning, lightning and rain.

Then the plane went quiet. The left engine had died. The C-46 dipped to the left. The pilot ordered the passengers to dump the cargo and prepare to bail. As Myfelt and another passenger were chucking a ton and a half of equipment and supplies, Captain John Wadsworth, a flight surgeon, stepped into the cockpit and urged the pilot to return to Warazup rather than ditch the plane. The pilot agreed and turned back. Myfelt secured himself with a cargo strap as the storm tossed and jerked the C-46.

The weather improved, but they weren't out of danger yet. A radio beam helped the pilot find the Warazup airstrip. But there was a problem: The airstrip had no lights.

He radioed the base that he was going to make an emergency landing. They dispatched a signalman to guide the plane and placed a

The plane went quiet.

There was a problem: The airstrip had no lights.

jeep at the end of the strip with its headlights on. The signalman had a green light and a red light. He would flash the red one if the plane wasn't low enough to land, the green one if he saw no problems.

As the C-46 came down, the green light flashed. All clear. The landing was bumpy, but no one was hurt.

★

THE NEXT DAY, A DIFFERENT CREW FLEW MYFELT AND HIS COMRADES TO Kunming in a Douglas C-47, a smaller craft than the C-46. It flew over the Himalayas without incident. The next evening, the same crew and passengers took off for Chungking in good weather.

After an hour, the pilot came over the intercom: "I'm getting some ice; you better put the chutes on." Ice not only added weight but also affected airflow over the wings, reducing their ability to remain airborne. The pilot climbed higher to avoid the ice, ascending from 10,000 to 15,000 feet. Ice was still forming on the plane. He went up to 20,000 feet, but even at that altitude ice kept forming. Passengers shared an oxygen bottle in order to breathe. No matter where he flew, the pilot couldn't find an altitude where ice didn't threaten to knock them out of the air.

"I'm going to have to bring it down," he said. Everyone remained calm and quiet.

Passengers shared an oxygen bottle in order to breathe.

They were near an emergency airstrip that fighters used. It didn't operate at night, though, which meant the pilot couldn't radio anyone at the base to help him land. It also meant the airstrip wouldn't have any lights.

The pilot brought the plane down. It rolled past the end of the short airstrip and stopped suddenly in a shallow rice paddy. The seat straps were meant for cargo, not humans, so the rough landing tossed the passengers around. Myfelt's ribs ached.

A jeep drove out to the rice paddy. A member of the base's medical corps bandaged Myfelt's ribs. He was thankful to have walked away from two rough flights in three days, but what next? He feared his luck was running out.

He made it to Hanchung without further incident and continued his cryptography work. At the end of the war with Japan, he was transferred back to Chungking, where he attended a lunch hosted by Generalissimo Chiang Kai-shek, China's Nationalist leader, to honor Americans who had served in squadrons against the Japanese. From Chungking, Myfelt went to Shanghai, where he did communications work. In mid-December 1945, he stepped onto the USS *General H. L. Scott*, which sailed eastward, arriving at Seattle on New Year's Eve.

Myfelt walked off the ship the next morning and into 1946. His first New Year's resolution was to find a restaurant and order something he sorely missed. He sat down and guzzled a chocolate milk shake.

Discharged in mid-January, Myfelt studied mathematics and science

He sat down and guzzled a chocolate milk shake.

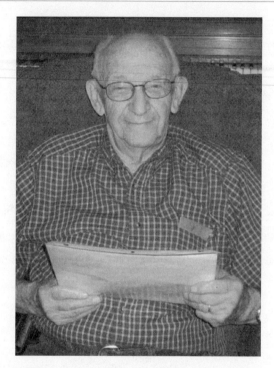

In 2012, George Myfelt looks at a photo of Generalissimo Chiang Kai-shek taken at a lunch that Myfelt attended to honor Americans who helped China during the war.

at Mansfield University, then attended Penn State for graduate work. He became an educator and worked as a teacher and administrator in Corning, New York.

"In the end, nobody wins in a war," he said, looking back.

SNAPSHOT OF WAR

GEORGE MCGOVERN

Second Lieutenant

741st Squadron

455th Bomb Group

Fifteenth Air Force

US Army Air Forces

E VERY TIME GEORGE MCGOVERN CLIMBED INTO THE COCKPIT OF his B-24 Liberator, the *Dakota Queen*, he placed a small photo of his wife, Eleanor, above the throttles on the instrument panel. She was the real Dakota queen. She had trounced him in a debating competition in high school, but now she represented his future— provided that he lived to see the end of the war. They had married before he left Mitchell, South Dakota, to serve with the Fifteenth Air Force in Cerignola, in southern Italy. A pilot with the 741st Squadron of the 455th Bomb Group, McGovern was twenty-two years old.

★

ON DECEMBER 20, 1944, ORDERS CAME IN FOR THE *DAKOTA QUEEN* AND THE thirty-six other bombers of the 455th. They were to target Skoda

George McGovern brought this photo of his wife, Eleanor, with him on his flights.

Works, an armaments manufac- turer for the German forces in Pilsen, Czechoslovakia. The intelligence officer at the preflight briefing warned them to expect heavy flak.

McGovern placed the photo of Eleanor, now pregnant with their first child, on his instrument panel. He looked through the cockpit window. Scattered clouds flecked the sky. He and copilot Lieutenant Bill Rounds took off at 7:30 a.m.

About an hour from Pilsen, at about 25,000 feet, the number two engine—inner left—developed a problem. The oil gauge showed that the pressure was dropping. But a B-24 could fly on three engines, so McGovern didn't worry. He feathered the propeller of the dying engine to turn the powerless blades sideways and prevent windmilling. To compensate, he increased the power in the other three engines.

Just before they arrived at their target, the *Dakota Queen* lurched. Shrapnel hit the number three engine—inner right—and it started smoking. McGovern tried to feather the prop, but it didn't work.

Lieutenant Sam Adams, the navigator, released their payload—ten 500-pound bombs. Moments later, the number three engine started vibrating. Flames flickered out of it. McGovern tried to feather the prop again, but it spun like a windmill, putting stress on the remaining engines.

The *Dakota Queen* began losing speed and altitude. McGovern radioed the squadron's lead plane. "This is Lieutenant McGovern in number three. I'm going to have to drop out," he said, referring to his formation position. Cerignola lay six hundred miles away.

Flames could burn through an engine's firewall in five minutes. If fire ignited the fuel tanks in the wings, they would explode.

McGovern lowered the nose of the plane and dived. The rush of air extinguished the fire, but the number three prop kept windmilling, reducing their speed.

"Prepare to bail out," he radioed his crew.

Sergeant Bill Ashlock, the waist gunner, was sitting at the escape

---

If fire ignited the fuel tanks in the wings, they would explode.

---

hatch near his station, his legs dangling out. A few long, agonizing minutes crawled by, and McGovern tried the feathering button one more time. The propellers turned sideways and stopped windmilling.

"Resume your stations," McGovern said.

Ashlock breathed a sigh of relief that they didn't have to bail. Adams, the navigator, set a southeasterly course to avoid German flak, then westward across the Adriatic to Cerignola. McGovern wasn't sure the *Dakota Queen* could make it back to base. He asked Adams whether he knew of any closer runways where they could land.

Nothing ideal, but Adams remembered Vis. McGovern had heard of the island, but he didn't know much about the runway there. Britain's Royal Air Force operated the airstrip, but the Partisans, the Yugoslav anti-Nazi resistance, controlled the island. The RAF primarily used the base for fighter planes like the Spitfire because the runway stretched just 2,200 feet—less than half the length that heavy bombers required—and a small mountain rose up at the end of it.

To reduce the *Dakota Queen*'s load, McGovern asked the crew to toss anything loose or easily removable. "Get rid of everything, even machine guns," he said over the intercom. The crew jettisoned machine guns and ammunition, flak suits and oxygen tanks.

That mountain meant McGovern couldn't circle around and make a second attempt. He had to make a perfect landing on his first approach. Flames suddenly shot from the number three engine again, but McGovern cut the fuel to all engines, and the fire went out. Looking

"Get rid of everything, even machine guns."

He had to make a perfect landing on his first approach.

down at the runway, they could see what had happened when pilots made imperfect landings: The wreckage of planes lay at the base of the mountain.

As he approached, McGovern cut their speed as much as he could. Flying between 110 and 120 miles an hour, he lowered the wheels as soon as the *Dakota Queen* cast a shadow over the runway. He and Rounds practically stood on their brakes, pressing them as hard as they could. The plane screeched along, racing closer and closer to the mountain. The *Dakota Queen* reached the end of the runway and rolled through twenty feet of wet clay before stopping.

Everyone walked off the plane, elated. They had survived. Some of them kissed the ground. Sergeant Mike Valko, the engineer, didn't fly on several subsequent flights. McGovern hugged Rounds. He was one day closer to seeing Eleanor again.

For the skill he demonstrated when flying to Vis, McGovern received the Distinguished Flying Cross. Another B-24 that landed shortly after the *Dakota Queen* didn't fare so well. It struck the mountain, killing everyone on board.

Another B-24 struck the mountain, killing everyone on board.

★

ON MARCH 14, 1945, ON A FLIGHT TO WIENER NEUSTADT IN AUSTRIA, about thirty miles south of Vienna, a bomb got stuck in the bomb rack of the *Dakota Queen*. As the plane approached the Italian border, the crew dislodged it, but McGovern saw the bomb hit a farmhouse below them and explode. It was noon. McGovern feared the farmer and his family were in the house eating lunch. He dreaded that they had killed an innocent family. Later that day, he learned that his daughter Ann had been born four days earlier.

★

BY THE SPRING OF 1945, THE ALLIES WERE CLOSE TO WINNING THE WAR IN Europe, but German anti-aircraft guns still posed a deadly threat to Allied bomber crews. On April 25, bombers from the 455th set out for Linz, Austria, a major rail center. At a preflight briefing, the intelligence officer warned that the Germans had amassed anti-aircraft guns in the city and that flak would likely be heavy.

The *Dakota Queen* took off at about 7 a.m. into a clear sky above beautiful lakes, trees, and mountains. But as the plane approached Linz, flak fired from the anti-aircraft guns created a horrible black cloud over the city. Red flashes from fresh shells streaked through the clouds. They had to fly straight through it.

Dozens of pieces of flak punched small holes in the fuselage and wings. Despite the barrage, McGovern flew directly over their target, and the crew dropped their load of 500-pound bombs.

Red flashes from fresh shells streaked through the clouds.

A piece of flak struck Ashlock, the waist gunner, in the left leg. Sergeant Ken Higgins, the radio operator, put sulfa powder and a bandage on Ashlock's wound. He also offered him a morphine injection, but Ashlock refused. He wanted to be fully alert.

Another piece of flak severed the hydraulic lines. Without hydraulic fluid, the brakes and wing flaps wouldn't work. Lieutenant Carroll Cooper, the navigator (who replaced Adams, who had died while flying with another crew), tried to collect some of the fluid in a helmet, but the lines were damaged so badly that they couldn't use it.

The men started shouting on the intercom.

"Take it easy. Take it easy," McGovern said. "We're going to be okay." He asked Valko, the engineer, to check the plane. The loss of hydraulic fluid was their biggest problem.

Flak had damaged the number three engine. McGovern feathered the propeller, and the *Dakota Queen* fell behind the formation. He discussed his options with Rounds and Cooper. Either they could fly back to Cerignola or turn eastward toward Soviet-held territory and hope to land there. Their plane was still flying—miraculously—so McGovern aimed for their base. This way, the crew had the option of parachuting out if they didn't want to risk landing in a severely damaged plane. But no one chose to bail. Everyone trusted that McGovern could bring them home safely, as he had always done.

Everyone trusted that McGovern could bring them home safely, as he had always done.

Closer to the base, he informed the control tower of the plane's condition. The brakes were inoperable, so they needed a way to slow the plane on landing. The crew manually lowered the wheels with a hand crank. Higgins, the radio operator, and Sergeant Bill McAfee, the ball-turret gunner, attached parachutes to girders at the waist gunners' positions. McGovern instructed the two men to throw the chutes from the aircraft as soon as the wheels kissed the runway. Everyone except Ashlock, who was injured, and Rounds, the copilot, would move into the tail section to add weight so that the rear wheel hit the runway more quickly, cutting the plane's speed.

The plan worked, but the aircraft rolled off the runway and dropped into a ditch. The tail rose up, then came down hard. Three members of the crew needed medical care. Ashlock required treatment for his leg; Cooper had sprained an ankle when the *Dakota Queen* finally stopped; and Valko sustained serious emotional trauma from the flak attack.

Mechanics found 110 holes in the *Dakota Queen*, but they patched her up, and she flew again. McGovern had saved American taxpayers the cost of replacing a $350,000 aircraft. He was relieved. That flight to Linz was not only his toughest, it was also his last: number thirty-five, the number required for a combat tour. Now he could return home and see his wife and baby daughter in person.

Mechanics found 110 holes in the *Dakota Queen*.

★

GEORGE MCGOVERN REENROLLED AT DAKOTA WESLEYAN UNIVERSITY, which he had left in 1943 to join the Army Air Forces. After earning his undergraduate degree, he attended seminary school at Northwestern University in Evanston, Illinois. Deciding not to become a minister, he took graduate courses in history at Northwestern and returned to Dakota Wesleyan in 1950 to teach. In 1956, he ran successfully for a seat in the House of Representatives and later served in the Senate.

More than a decade later, deeply concerned about the war in Vietnam, McGovern accepted the Democratic Party's nomination to run for president. He vigorously opposed the war and didn't think the communist government of North Vietnam posed the type of threat to America that Nazi Germany or Imperial Japan had. During the campaign, the right-wing John Birch Society published an article that expressed skepticism about McGovern's war record, accusing him of cowardice. His crew vehemently refuted the allegations and praised their pilot's courage and skill. Bill Ashlock, the waist gunner, further supported his former pilot by serving as cochairman of the McGovern campaign in Santa Clara County, California. McGovern won only Massachusetts and the District of Columbia in the general election, but two years later, President Nixon, embroiled in the Watergate scandal, resigned the presidency.

President Barack Obama called him a hero of war who became a champion of peace.

Despite his opposition to America's policies in Vietnam, McGovern never considered himself a pacifist and didn't regret flying a bomber during World War II.

"I never had a moment's doubt about the American cause, the Allied cause," he said. During World War II, unlike the Vietnam War, the United States was "totally committed."

His ordeals as a B-24 pilot made him appreciate that death of any kind lurks constantly in a war zone. He urged America's political leaders to pause before sending troops off to war. "The ordinary people of the world have little to say about going to war. War should always be regarded as a last recourse."

Long after the war, he learned through a television program that no one had been in the farmhouse that his crew inadvertently bombed on March 14, 1945. The farmer had seen the B-24 coming and gotten his family out of the house in time.

McGovern didn't dwell on his wartime activities, nor did he ever forget the woman who had inspired him. She died in 2007, but he kept that same snapshot that he brought with him on those thirty-five combat flights on the living room wall of his home in St. Augustine, Florida.

George McGovern died in 2012 at the age of ninety. In a statement from the White House, President Barack Obama called him a hero of war who became a champion of peace.

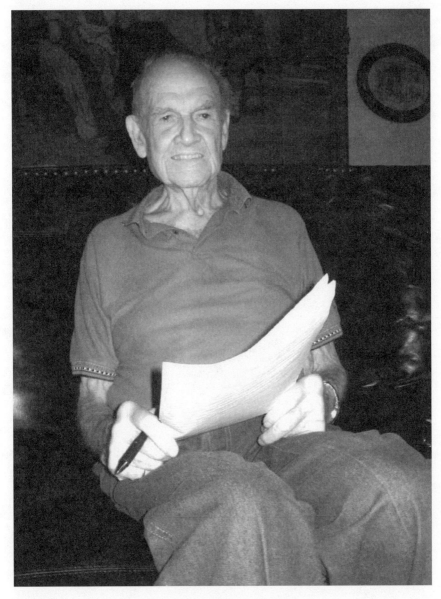

George McGovern reviews an article that he was writing in 2012.

AFTERWORD

FROM WAR TO PEACE

N THE FIRST CHAPTER OF THIS BOOK, "SHOCKWAVES," JIM LANDIS TOOK a bullet through his left hand and then climbed into a plane to fire back at the Japanese aircraft attacking Pearl Harbor. He personified America's indomitable spirit on December 7, 1941. There was simply no question that he, like the nation, would fight back.

Military historians may forever debate the details of the attack, but there is no debate about its consequences. America was a nation divided on December 6, 1941, but the isolationist movement, which had been lobbying fiercely to keep America out of the war, all but dissolved before the fires in Hawaii were extinguished. On December 8, practically everyone put aside their differences and did what was necessary to win the war against the Axis powers.

President Roosevelt was right. December 7 continues to live in infamy. Each year, even decades later, it reminds us that we live in a fragile world and to appreciate the sacrifices made by the veterans of World War II as well as those who served in other conflicts since. The world remains an imperfect place, but we all can agree that it would have become immeasurably worse if the Allies hadn't defeated Nazi Germany, Imperial Japan, and Fascist Italy.

Winston Churchill, Britain's wartime prime minister, understood the significance of America joining the Allies. As he revealed in *The Second World War: The Grand Alliance*, he came to an immediate conclusion: "So we had won after all!" Tragically and fatally, though, German and Japanese leaders lacked Churchill's foresight. They underestimated the determination of America and its allies. That shortsightedness ultimately cost the lives of millions of men, women, and children on both sides.

Tom Lane—a Canadian pilot whose wartime ordeal appears in *Amazing Airmen*, my collection of stories about Canadian fliers— saw the American determination to win the war. When he talked to American airmen in Britain, he understood what Churchill thought on December 7, 1941. Lane, the pilot who flew with one of my uncles, saw their vitality, energy, concentration, and intensity. "They weren't going to lose this one," he said, and I saw these traits in every American veteran I interviewed.

★

THE DEVELOPMENT OF THE ATOMIC BOMB REMAINED A WELL-GUARDED military secret until August 6, 1945, the day the *Enola Gay* flew from Tinian Island to drop "Little Boy" on Hiroshima. Before that flight, Tom Taterka, a B-29 radio operator and navigator based on the island, talked to Colonel Paul Tibbets, the pilot of the *Enola Gay*. Tibbets told him that crews such as his were going to end the war, but he didn't say how. Taterka did notice, though, that the bomb bay doors on Tibbets's plane were different from those on other B-29s. They were bigger.

Taterka first heard about Hiroshima while flying back to Tinian from a bombing mission over Japan. He learned that a special bomb had been dropped on the city. At first, he didn't realize how different the bomb had been. A few days later, he and his crew were flying near Nagasaki after Major Charles Sweeney, captain of the *Bockscar* B-29, had dropped "Fat Man" on the seaport. A cloud rose up from the city. "It was big," Taterka said, hoping that the bombs would force the Japanese government to surrender.

It did, and the war against Japan came to a swift end. President Truman regretted the massive loss of life, but he had decided to use those powerful weapons to end the war as quickly as he could. He knew that an invasion of Japan would cost the lives of thousands more American soldiers.

The atomic bombs remain a controversial subject in Japan. Many Japanese want the American government to apologize for using them, which it hasn't done. President Truman's grandson Clifton Truman Daniel—who went to Japan in 2012 to help the postwar reconciliation process—started thinking of going there after his son brought home a book about a girl in Hiroshima who died from cancer caused by radiation produced by the atomic bomb. As he pointed out in the foreword, whether you count the decision as right or wrong, his grandfather made it to save the lives of Americans such as those whose stories appear in this book. All the veterans interviewed for this book looked back with pride at what they and their comrades accomplished. Their sacrifices and others' achieved a greater goal: Never again has Germany or

Japan threatened America or its allies. The veterans didn't help win the war; they helped win the peace. Indeed, many often expressed pleasant surprise at the speed with which Germany and Japan became democratic countries.

After World War I, the harsh terms imposed on Germany by the Treaty of Versailles demonstrated that severe punishment could have severe consequences. The Allied decision not to punish the people of the Axis countries undoubtedly helped create a more peaceful world. Among other programs and initiatives, the Marshall Plan, which helped European countries rebuild their economies, symbolized that postwar goodwill.

As the stories in this book illustrate, the veterans of World War II have left us a legacy that we must never forget. They stayed calm during times of crisis, they thought of their comrades before they thought of themselves, and they remained modest about their accomplishments. By remembering and celebrating these ideals, we not only honor these veterans, we better prepare ourselves to meet the challenges ahead.

ACKNOWLEDGMENTS

M Y NAME APPEARS ON THE JACKET OF THIS BOOK, BUT, FOR A collection of stories such as these, that gives a distorted impression of the way *Heroes in the Skies* evolved. These stories aren't really mine; they belong to the men and women who survived these harrowing ordeals. I have tried below to thank everyone who assisted me as I researched and wrote this book, so I offer a sincere apology to anyone I have overlooked inadvertently.

Several people, including members of my family, helped with many stories. My wife, Jane Ann McLachlan, and two of my daughters, Amanda and Caroline, read drafts of numerous chapters and offered their advice. My daughter Tamara and her husband, Steve Amirault, looked after backup copies of significant notes I took while researching the veterans' ordeals.

Rob Wilson, a former colleague at the *Waterloo Region Record*, read many stories and offered comments based on his deep knowledge of World War II.

After I decided to write about American veterans, Marilyn Walton, author, researcher, and organizer of Stalag Luft III reunions, was one of the first people I contacted. I am particularly grateful that she invited me to a joint reunion in Detroit in 2010 of members of the Eighth Air

Force and prisoners of war held at Stalag Luft III. I met several veterans through that reunion whom I later interviewed.

Holly Shelton of Pensacola, Florida, helped me contact three veterans after she saw a story I wrote in the *Pensacola News Journal*.

Dr. Dave Waldbillig, a neighbor and emergency-room physician in Kitchener, Ontario, helped me understand the medical problems that several veterans faced.

Manfred Kremer, as well as John and Anne Kroisenbrunner, assisted by translating some German phrases.

I thank Clifton Truman Daniel for writing the foreword. I contacted him after learning that he went to Hiroshima to promote the reconciliation process between America and Japan. His interest in this subject prompted him to write about the survivors of the atomic bombs dropped on Japan.

I also thank James Jayo, the editor at Sterling Publishing who looked after *Heroes in the Skies*. I very much appreciate the interest he took in my book, as well as his wise and helpful advice.

NOTES

CHAPTER 1: SHOCKWAVES

I first heard about Jim Landis through Holly Shelton, who had seen a story I wrote about John Raiser. Holly wondered whether I wanted to write about Landis. To this day, I have never heard of anyone else who did what Landis did.

Tex and Gloria Hill, Landis's neighbors, provided background on his ordeal. Dr. Dave Waldbillig explained how Landis could continue firing despite his injury.

Ole Griffith helped me meet Harold Snider. I also appreciated an article Snider wrote with the assistance of Griffith and Graham Smith for a newsletter at Snider's retirement home in Phoenix.

Ken DeHoff, executive director of the Pacific Aviation Museum Pearl Harbor on Ford Island, and Burl Burlingame, the museum's curator, helped me better understand what happened on Ford Island on December 7, 1941.

Jim Neuman, a historian at Navy Region Hawaii, along with Second Lieutenant Jessica Colby, Technical Sergeant Anthony Gomez, Paul Hibbeln, and Dave Underwood, provided background about the attack on Pearl Harbor and Hickam Field.

Robert Cressman, a historian at the Naval History and Heritage Command, provided information on damaged planes. The command's website, www.navy.mil/local /navhist/, contains useful, detailed information on the attack.

Two books also provided general background for this chapter: *7 December 1941: The Air Force Story*, by Leatrice R. Arakaki and John R. Kuborn; and *The First Team: Pacific Naval Air Combat from Pearl Harbor to Midway*, by John B. Lundstrom. Information about Mitsuo Fuchida's conversion to Christianity came from *God's Samurai: Lead Pilot at Pearl Harbor*, by Gordon W. Prange, Donald M. Goldstein, and Katherine V. Dillon. Details of the attack on the air bases in Hawaii come from a fact sheet prepared by the Fifteenth Wing of the US Air Force.

CHAPTER 2: THE VOLUNTEER

The Doolittle Raid showed that Japan was more vulnerable and less isolated than many Japanese may have wished or as many Americans may have feared.

Thanks to Tom Casey, the Raiders' manager, I met one of the participants in the raid. Casey put me in touch with Ray Hughes, who arranged for me to meet his friend Tom Griffin, a Raider who lived in Cincinnati.

Much has been written about the raid, including General James Doolittle's auto-biography, *I Could Never Be So Lucky Again*, which provided good background information, as did the Doolittle Raiders' official website, doolittleraider.com.

Additional helpful sources include two articles by Kevin C. McHugh in the Cincinnati Historical Society's journal: "Queen City Heritage: Navigating from Shangri-La: Cincinnati's Doolittle Raider at War," and "Above and Beyond: Cincinnati's Doolittle Raider in Europe." Also useful were *Flak Bait: The Story of the B-26 Bombers and the Men Who Flew Them in World War II*, by Devon Francis, and "Back from Hell," by Burris Jenkins Jr., which appeared in the *Milwaukee Sentinel* on August 6, 1943, and describes the attack by *Hell's Cargo* on a freighter.

CHAPTER 3: THE FLYING FORTRESS

Dr. Charles Bateman first told me about the *All American* and its ability to fly despite sustaining severe damage.

Sam Silvey, a nephew of Ralph Burbridge, the bombardier on the *All American*, helped me contact Burbridge and his wife, Peggy, as well as Silvey's brother, Larry, who was also interested in his uncle's experience. Peggy sent me information about the incident as well.

Aura Bragg, wife of Kendrick Bragg, the pilot of the *All American*, sent me a pamphlet about her husband.

Margaret Johnson provided information about her uncle Charles "Cliff" Cutforth, who took what became a famous photo of the *All American*.

CHAPTER 4: WHITE CLIFFS

Peter Chamberlain, the director of sales at Publishers' Design and Production Services in Sagamore Beach, Massachusetts, helped me contact Robert Patterson. Patterson's daughter Lynn Pasko not only gave me information about her father's ordeal but also asked him questions on my behalf. A booklet on Patterson's military career by Terry Ruggles, a resident of Cape Cod, was also helpful. Lynn's sister, Catherine Nass, sent photos of their father.

Hunter Chaney, director of marketing for the Collings Foundation, which operates the Wings of Freedom Tour, told me about the website created by the 303rd Bomb Group association, www.303rdbg.com, a source for information about ditching a B-17.

The website of the Eighth Air Force Historical Society, 8thafhs.org, contains the full names of all the members of Patterson's crew.

CHAPTER 5: A LONG WAY TO BRADENTON

Russell Jones introduced me to the story of Jim Armstrong's experience. Armstrong and Jones had been evaders together.

My lengthy interviews with Armstrong—and his book, *Escape!*, about his ordeal that started when he was shot down over France—served as important sources for the chapter.

Michael LeBlanc, a Canadian who has studied Allied evaders and members of the Resistance who helped them, identified Gilbert Virmoux, whom Armstrong knew during the war only by his first name.

CHAPTER 6: LOCKED IN PLACE

Holly Shelton first told me about Betty Guild, later Betty Blake. Thanks also to Peg Sheridan, Louise Van Vliet, and Roxanne Cottrell.

Cee John, manager of the National Aviation Hall of Fame in Dayton, Ohio, helped me contact Barbara Erickson London, the commander of the Women's Auxiliary Ferrying Squadron at Long Beach, California. Betty Darst and Sarah Rickman contacted Barbara's daughter, Terry Rinehart, on my behalf. Terry and her daughter, Kelly, enabled me to put questions to Barbara.

The National Museum of the United States Air Force at Dayton has an excellent exhibit about the women fliers and an enlightening video, *Flying for Freedom*.

Wingtip to Wingtip: 8 WASPs, by Marjorie H. Roberts, includes a chapter on Betty.

CHAPTER 7: THE SALUTE

"The Salute" appeared in slightly different form in my Canadian book, *Amazing Airmen: Canadian Flyers in the Second World War*, published by Dundurn Press of Toronto. My thanks to them for permitting me to use the chapter in this book.

Charles Brown gave me a copy of *Raiders of the Reich*, by Martin W. Bowman and Theo Boiten, in which Brown wrote about his encounter with Franz Stigler.

Stigler's wife, Helga, helpfully answered questions on behalf of her husband when he became ill.

CHAPTER 8: NATURAL FLYER

Bruce Martin told me about Robert Querns. When I contacted Querns, I learned that he had survived five episodes, any one of which could have been disastrous. A remarkable record.

CHAPTER 9: DREAMING OF TROUBLE

Wilf Renner told me about Charles Warren. They had been evaders together in Belgium.

Warren learned about Lieutenant Ivo von Lubich-Edler Milowa, the German pilot who shot down *Roarin' Bill*, when he met Nicolas Clinaz, a Belgian researcher. Clinaz wrote about the attack in a Belgian historical booklet, *Le Lothier Roman*.

Warren, a tail gunner, learned about the shell that hit the cockpit from Second Lieutenant David O'Boyle, the navigator, at a reunion of the Air Forces Escape and Evasion Society in May 1988 in Denver.

CHAPTER 10: BULLDOGS OF THE AIR

In Detroit in 2010, I met Frank Buschmeier and his two sons, Michael and William, at a joint reunion of veterans from the Eighth Air Force and men held prisoner at Stalag Luft III. Buschmeier told me he had flown a plane called *Miss Irish*, which had been badly damaged. Buschmeier's daughter, Nancy Brennan, later helped me keep in contact with her father.

Pilot John Gibbons provided more information about the flight in a phone interview. He also gave me a photo of *Miss Irish*.

Additional background information on the flight came from an article in *8th AF News* magazine in June 2010.

CHAPTER 11: SURPRISE FLIGHT

I was able to talk to paratrooper Sidney Richard thanks to Tex Hill of Pensacola, who had met Richard at the Naval Air Museum. *On to Berlin*, by Richard's commander, Brigadier General James M. Gavin, helped me learn about the paratroopers who landed behind the Normandy beaches.

The Airborne Museum in Sainte-Mère-Église, France, has an excellent video about the airborne invasion on its website, www.airborne-museum.org/en/. A page on the website also mentions paratrooper John Steele, whose parachute caught on a church steeple. Steele's unusual landing also appears in an exhibit at the Armed Forces History Museum in Largo, Florida. Thanks to Cindy Bosselmann, the museum's assistant executive director.

CHAPTER 12: REMEMBERING A FRIEND

I met Allen Jones in Detroit in 2010 at a joint reunion of members of the Eighth Air Force and prisoners of war from Stalag Luft III. Jones's grandson, Thomas Jones, who accompanied him, and Jones's daughter, Sarah Strange, helped me stay in contact with him.

I also spoke on the phone with Harry Walz, the tail gunner on Jones's plane.

CHAPTER 13: SIX CREWMATES

I met John Raiser at the Eighth Air Force/Stalag Luft III reunion.

Edouard Renière, a Belgian researcher who attended the reunion, translated the Web page of a Dutch museum, Wings to Victory, about Raiser's flight (wingstovictory .nl/).

Nick Ursiak's sons, David and Nick Jr., provided information about their father, who was on the forced march with Raiser.

Dr. Dave Waldbillig helped me understand how Raiser could pull his ripcord with an injured arm.

In 2011, the *Pensacola News Journal* published a short version of Raiser's story that I had written. The favorable response encouraged me to continue interviewing American veterans.

CHAPTER 14: SOFT LANDING

Andy Frederick, a member of the 352nd Fighter Group Association, told me about Bob Powell's experience.

EAA Video Player has a fine video in which Powell speaks about his wartime service in general and in particular about his emergency landing: www.eaavideo.org /video.aspx?v=16883825001.

Steve Jebson, a library information officer at the UK Met Office, provided details about the weather on the day of Powell's incident.

CHAPTER 15: THE COLOR BARRIER

Marilyn Walton, author, researcher, and organizer of Stalag Luft III reunions, helped me contact Alex Jefferson.

Red Tail Captured, Red Tail Free, by Jefferson, describes not only his wartime ordeals but also the discrimination that the Tuskegee Airmen faced.

Thanks to Joe Caver, chief of circulations at the Air Force Historical Research Agency at Maxwell Air Force Base in Montgomery, Alabama, for background information about the Tuskegee Airmen.

CHAPTER 16: MISSION TO REMEMBER

Thanks to the assistance of President George H. W. Bush's office in Houston and the George Bush Presidential Library in College Station, Texas.

All the Best: My Life in Letters and Other Writings, by George H. W. Bush, served as an excellent source of information about his ordeal and includes the letter he wrote to his parents the following day. Even given the restrictions of wartime censorship, it explains how Bush got out of the Avenger and the responsibility he felt for the fate of his two crewmates.

Looking Forward, by President Bush with Victor Gold, contains a good description of Bush's ordeal in his own words. *Heartbeat: George Bush in His Own Words*, compiled and edited by Jim McGrath, contains Bush's comments at the funeral of Emperor Hirohito and to veterans on the fiftieth anniversary of the attack on Pearl Harbor. Bush also mentions that he considered joining the Royal Canadian Air Force.

Bush describes how his wartime experiences affected his future thinking in his foreword, written with Hugh Sidey, to *Absolute Victory: America's Greatest Generation and Their World War II Triumph*, by the editors of *Time*.

Also useful were *Barbara Bush: A Memoir*, by Barbara Bush; *My Father, My President: A Personal Account of the Life of George H. W. Bush*, by Doro Bush Koch; and the Naval History and Heritage Command's website.

Navy Wings of Gold, by F. Willard Robinson, presents Nathaniel Adams's account of Bush's experience. Adams flew in a Hellcat fighter to protect the Avenger from torpedo bombers that attacked the radio tower on Chichi Jima. Adams heard Bush tell his two crewmates to leave the plane.

Thanks again to the George Bush Presidential Library for the photos used in this chapter, including the photo of Bush parachuting, which was taken by Donna Dixon and provided courtesy of the US Army Golden Knights.

CHAPTER 17: THE MYSTERIOUS PILOT
Craig Johnson, pilot of the B-17 used in the movie *Memphis Belle*, told me about Bruce Martin.

Martin's friend Cora Goyette helped me arrange interview sessions.

Steve Blake, editor of the P-38 National Association publication *Lightning Strikes*, provided information about black pilots.

CHAPTER 18: IGNITION TROUBLE
Thanks to Holly Shelton for introducing me to Cass Phillips's story, which shows a crew reacting to sudden stress.

Dr. Dave Waldbillig helped me understand Phillips's physical reaction to the stress.

Jim Neuman, a historian at Navy Region Hawaii, provided statistical information.

CHAPTER 19: DEVOUT DUTY
Herman Echsner's son, Stephen, contacted me after he read my story about John Raiser that appeared in the *Pensacola News Journal*.

CHAPTER 20: MISS STEVE
Bill Barnhart and Bill Marshall, members of the 355th Fighter Group Association, helped me contact Bill Cullerton. Thanks also to Marshall for Cullerton's official war record as well as photos of him taken during the war.

Robert Garlich, another pilot in Cullerton's squadron, provided details of the attack on *Miss Steve* in a telephone interview.

The Window at St. Catherine's, by John F. Dobbertin Jr., provided helpful background about Cullerton's incident.

Dr. Dave Waldbillig helped me understand the wound Cullerton suffered when a Waffen-SS officer fired at him.

CHAPTER 21: FIGHTING THE WEATHER
John Wright told me about George Myfelt, whom he'd met at a vintage car rally.

The Burma Bridge Busters, by Howard Bell and Anthony Strotman, provided background on Myfelt's squadron.

CHAPTER 22: SNAPSHOT OF WAR
At a reunion of former prisoners of war in Detroit, Carl Loiocano told me that George McGovern had been a member of his squadron, the 741st Squadron of the 455th Bomb Group. Donald Simmons, dean of the College of Public Service, Leadership, and Graduate Studies at Dakota Wesleyan University in Mitchell, South Dakota, helped me contact the former senator. Thanks also to McGovern's daughter Ann.

Thanks to the assistance of Laurie Langland, the archivist at Dakota Wesleyan University, which holds the McGovern archives. The archives provided the two photos of Mrs. McGovern: pinning wings on her husband and the one that he always took on his flights.

Bill Ashlock, waist gunner on McGovern's crew, helped clarify details of the crew's ordeals during several phone interviews.

McGovern's autobiography, *Grassroots*, contains particularly helpful information about his wartime experiences. *The Wild Blue*, by Stephen Ambrose, provided background information for my interview with McGovern at his winter home in St. Augustine, Florida.

Thanks to several members of the 455th Bomb Group association, including Craig Ward, John Rohrer, and Greg Riggs.

Background on the 1972 presidential election: "Crew Is Split on Politics, Not George" by Daryl Lembke, *Los Angeles Times*, October 14, 1972.

AFTERWORD: FROM WAR TO PEACE

Tom Lane, a Canadian pilot who served on the same RAF crew as my uncle, told me of the American resolve to win World War II. As a young boy, Manfred Kremer was in a German city that Lane's crew bombed and enabled me to understand the postwar reconciliation process better.

Gus Hawkins, a volunteer at the Military Heritage Museum in Punta Gorda, Florida, posed questions on my behalf to David Lee, a former B-25 pilot, in Schererville, Indiana.

Carl Brunsberg helped me contact Tom Taterka, a veteran in South St. Paul, Minnesota, who had spoken to Paul Tibbets, the pilot of the *Enola Gay*.

The Second World War: The Grand Alliance, by Winston Churchill, was indispensable.

PHOTO CREDITS

Senator George McGovern Collection, Dakota Wesleyan University
Archives, Dakota Wesleyan University, Mitchell, South Dakota:
255, 256

George Myfelt: 249

Catherine Nass: 41, 45

National Archives: vii

Cass Phillips: 223

Bob Powell: 185

Robert Querns: 107

Jack Raiser: 173

Sidney Richard: 149

Larry Silvey: 39

Harold Snider: 9

Charles Warren: 117

INDEX

Pages in *italics* contain photos